GOOD HOUSEKEEPING
Best Menus

FOOD AND WINE
FOR ALL OCCASIONS

EBURY PRESS LONDON

Published by Ebury Press
Division of The National Magazine Company Ltd
Colquhoun House
27–37 Broadwick Street
London W1V 1FR

First impression 1988

ISBN 0 85223 639 5

Designed by Roger Daniels
Wine notes by Jane MacQuitty
Recipes by Caroline Richmond Walker, Fiona Oyston,
Carol Miller and Sue Ross of the Good Housekeeping Institute
Cover photograph by Peter Myers

Filmset by Advanced Filmsetters (Glasgow) Ltd

Printed and bound in Italy by New Interlitho S.p.a., Milan

Photographs by
Martin Brigdale
Laurie Evans
Graham Kirk
Peter Myers
Charlie Stebbings
Clive Streeter
Simon Wheeler
Andrew Whittock

CONTENTS

INTRODUCTION

Good Housekeeping Best Menus is designed to take the stress out of entertaining – no more evenings spent quietly panicking in the kitchen while your guests make polite conversation, wondering in what form disaster has struck this time.

This book contains twenty complete menus to suit a variety of different occasions. There are suggestions for both formal and informal entertaining, indoor and outdoor meals, late night suppers and family lunches. Each menu provides a complete blueprint for each meal – from detailed recipes for each course to wine suggestions and a comprehensive failsafe countdown plan.

We have included a selection of different cuisines to tempt every palate. The French supper for four comprises four delicious, authentic recipes from Northern France, while the Middle Eastern dinner reflects the many influences of the region's rich and complicated history. The Chinese menu brings an oriental flavour to the kitchen and encourages you to experiment with different cooking methods. Traditional English fare is represented by a full Sunday lunch for twelve – the ideal meal for a family get-together.

The menus are divided into seasons, making the most of produce when it is at its very best. Light buffet-style meals can be served during the summer months – ideal for eating in the garden – while hearty, warming dishes can be prepared for the winter evenings.

Each menu is accompanied by comprehensive wine notes, compiled by Jane MacQuitty, *Good Housekeeping* magazine's wine editor. A selection of wines covering a wide range of prices are suggested to complement each course.

To avoid any last minute panic or a long wait between courses, we have drawn up an invaluable countdown plan for each menu. This provides an easy-to-follow timetable for action in the kitchen, from preparation the day before the dinner party, right up to five minutes before your guests arrive, thus ensuring that everything is cooked to perfection, and that you can relax.

Good Housekeeping Best Menus will turn entertaining your friends from a chore into an enjoyable occasion and help you give dinner parties that cannot fail to impress.

SOPHISTICATED SPRING DINNER

Menu for Eight

CAULIFLOWER SOUFFLÉS

PARSLEY CHICKEN WITH CASHEW

SHREDDED CABBAGE WITH GARLIC

GLAZED TURNIPS

BROWN RICE

PAPAYA PIE

This dinner party cannot fail to impress your guests. Soufflés are remarkably easy, but never fail to delight. By preparing them in small dishes, you make the timing very easy – wait until your guests arrive, then whisk the egg whites and put the soufflés to bake. Chicken is such a good medium for all flavours. Here, we've gently simmered breast fillets with spices, coconut and parsley. The mildly aromatic taste is complemented by the slight sweetness of baby turnips and nutty brown rice. Papayas, or pawpaws as they're often called, are becoming easier to find now – many supermarkets and greengrocers stock them – and they keep their shape beautifully in Papaya Pie. Do serve this when just warm. The fragrant scent is lost if it's served too cold.

CAULIFLOWER SOUFFLÉS

These light, delicate soufflés are ideal to precede a substantial main dish. If the sauce base is left to cool before you complete the soufflés, bake for about 10 minutes longer.

225 g	small cauliflower florets	½ lb
	salt and pepper	
	Parmesan cheese	
	butter *or* polyunsaturated margarine	
45 ml	flour	3 level tbsp
200 ml	milk	7 fl oz
15 ml	wholegrain mustard	1 level tbsp
100 g	Gruyère cheese	4 oz
	4 eggs	

Just cover the cauliflower with salted water. Cover and simmer until tender; drain. Grease eight 150 ml (¼ pint) ramekin dishes; dust out with Parmesan.

Meanwhile, prepare a white sauce from 40 g (1½ oz) fat, the flour, milk, mustard and seasoning. Purée the sauce and cauliflower until almost smooth. Turn out into a large bowl, cool slightly. Stir in the grated Gruyère cheese with the egg yolks.

Whisk the egg whites until stiff but not dry and fold into the sauce mixture. Spoon into the dishes. Bake at 180°C (350°F) mark 4 for 25 minutes, or until well browned and firm to the touch. Serve immediately.

WINES WITH THE FOOD

While the murmurs of appreciation run round the table for the individual Cauliflower Soufflés dreamt up by the GH cooks, you will still want your guests to notice the wine. A tall order, for the soufflé has a strong taste both of Gruyère and cauliflower. If spring isn't far away, a positive, green, aromatic white wine that could double up as an aperitif is an ideal choice. The GH panel tried and rejected a prestigious Loire Sauvignon before opting for a very high-class Sylvaner from Alsace, whose firm, fresh, green, flowery herbaceous style copes easily with the soufflé. But be warned, most Alsace Sylvaners are nowhere near as positive as this well-made, reasonably priced wine from the Turckheim cooperative. As an alternative, try the excellent, moderately priced and widely available '85 Montana Sauvignon Blanc from New Zealand whose greeny-gold colour and intense, rich, tastebud-tingling, nettly style is a great favourite with GH.

On to the Parsley Chicken with Cashew, whose rich, softly spicy, cashew-laden sauce has a delicious hint of coconut. You could continue with the Montana Sauvignon but most of the panel preferred the splendid '81 Firestone Merlot from California with this dish, slightly more expensive, but good value. (Available from good wine merchants.) Its warm, spicy, plummy-fruity flavour made a perfect foil to the chicken and its sauce. Whatever your choice, avoid a European red with this dish; most will be wiped out by the sweet spicy sauce.

As for the pudding, a moreish Papaya Pie, the crisp cinnamon and orange pastry enclosing sweet, exotic-tasting papaya is perfectly matched by half-bottles of '80 Coutet with its luscious, peachy-pineapple taste. Alternatively, try a half-bottle of the Australian dessert wine, Brown Brothers Orange Muscat and Flora, with its strong, sweet, spicy flavour (from specialist outlets).

PARSLEY CHICKEN WITH CASHEW

50 g	creamed coconut	2 oz
	bunch fresh parsley	
225 g	onion	8 oz
100 g each	8 chicken breast fillets	4 oz each
60 ml	flour	4 level tbsp
30 ml	ground coriander	2 level tbsp
30 ml	cumin	2 level tbsp
10 ml	ground turmeric	2 level tsp
	salt and pepper	
	polyunsaturated oil	
25 g	butter	1 oz
150 g	salted cashew nuts	5 oz
600 ml	chicken stock	1 pint
60 ml	lemon juice	4 tbsp

Break up the coconut and dissolve in 150 ml ($\frac{1}{4}$ pint) boiling water. Chop the parsley to give about 90 ml (6 level tbsp). Slice the onion.

Split each chicken breast to give two thinner fillets. Mix together the flour, spices and seasoning. Use to coat the chicken.

Heat 60 ml (4 tbsp) oil and the butter in a large flameproof casserole or sauté pan. Brown the chicken pieces half at a time; remove from the pan. Add the onion and 125 g (4 oz) nuts with a little more oil if necessary and lightly brown, stirring frequently.

Mix in any remaining flour followed by the coconut, water, the stock, 75 ml (5 level tbsp) parsley and the lemon juice. Return the chicken to the pan. Bring to the boil, cover and simmer for about 20 minutes, or until the chicken is quite tender, stirring occasionally. Uncover and bubble down the juices until slightly thickened. Adjust seasoning and sprinkle with the remaining parsley and nuts.

MINIMAL CHIC FOR A STUDIO SUPPER

Menu for Six

GRAPEFRUIT AND CHICK PEA SALAD

VEAL AND BACON KEBABS

SPINACH AND MUSHROOM BAKE

GOLDEN POTATO THATCH

CHOCOLATE MOUSSE CAKE

*S*imple in presentation, though not quite so simple in preparation, this supper for six can be served anywhere – even in the kitchen. Ideal for gregarious eaters who like a dash of informality. The combination of pink grapefruit and chick peas makes an unusual and colourful starter, and you can be sure that the Chocolate Mousse Cake will become a firm favourite with all chocoholics!

GRAPEFRUIT AND CHICK PEA SALAD

A 396 g (14 oz) can of chick peas can be used to replace the dried ones. Look out for pink-fleshed grapefruit which adds pleasing colour to this salad.

125 g	chick peas	4 oz
	2 grapefruit	
45 ml	olive oil	3 tbsp
	pinch sugar	
	salt and pepper	
	½ bunch watercress	

Cover the chick peas well with cold water and leave to soak overnight. Drain, cover with fresh cold water and bring to the boil. Cover and boil until tender, about 1–1¼ hours.

Meanwhile, using a small serrated knife peel the grapefruit as you would an apple to remove all the peel and pith. Work over a bowl to catch all grapefruit juices. Segment the fruit discarding the membrane and halve any large segments. Cover and refrigerate. Whisk about 90 ml (6 tbsp) of the reserved grapefruit juices with the oil, sugar and seasoning.

Wash, drain and pat dry the watercress on kitchen paper; finely chop, discarding any hairy root ends. Stir into the dressing. When tender, drain the chick peas and immediately stir into the dressing. When quite cold, stir in the grapefruit segments. Cover tightly and refrigerate for a few hours.

Take the salad out of the refrigerator about 1 hour before serving. Taste for seasoning, adding a little more sugar if necessary.

VEAL AND BACON KEBABS

For all kebabs it's important to pack the skewers loosely so that the meat will cook through. Baste them frequently while grilling.

450 g	veal fillet in one piece	1 lb
225 g	streaky bacon	½ lb
	1 green pepper	
225 g	onion	½ lb
125 g	no-soak dried apricots	4 oz
	1 large orange	
150 ml	port *or* red wine	¼ pint
2.5 ml	dried thyme	½ level tsp
	salt and pepper	
5 ml	sugar	1 level tsp
5–10 ml	arrowroot	1–2 level tsp

Cut up the veal into small, bite-sized pieces. Snip the rind off the bacon; stretch each rasher with the back of a knife then divide in half. Roll up tightly. Cut the pepper

Minimal chic extends to the table decor; simple glass and plain china keep it stylish yet informal.

into 1 cm ($\frac{1}{2}$ in) squares, discarding the core and seeds; cut the onion into similar sized pieces. Thread the veal, bacon rolls, onion, pepper and apricots on to long metal or wooden skewers. Place the skewers in shallow dishes (*not* metal).

Mix the finely grated orange rind and orange juice with the port, 150 ml ($\frac{1}{4}$ pint) water, thyme and seasoning. If using wine stir in the sugar. Pour over the kebabs; cover with cling film and refrigerate for about 24 hours. Turn and baste occasionally.

Lift the kebabs out of the marinade and place on a grill pan. Grill for 15–20 minutes, in two batches if necessary, frequently turning and basting with a little marinade. Keep warm, loosely covered in a low oven. Mix half the arrowroot with a little water to form a smooth paste. Add to the remaining marinade and bring to the boil, stirring. Simmer for 1–2 minutes or until lightly thickened. (Add remaining arrowroot if necessary.) Adjust the seasoning and serve with kebabs.

Spinach and Mushroom Bake

This light spinach bake is best served straight from the oven – like all soufflé type mixtures it dries and shrinks on standing. It can be baked in individual dishes – cook for slightly less time.

1.4 kg	fresh spinach	3 lb
225 g	button mushrooms	$\frac{1}{2}$ lb
45 ml	polyunsaturated oil	3 tbsp
30 ml	flour	2 level tbsp
300 ml	milk	$\frac{1}{2}$ pint
10 ml	wholegrain mustard	2 level tsp
	salt and pepper	
	2 eggs	
50 g	fresh breadcrumbs	2 oz
	polyunsaturated margarine	

Discard the coarse spinach stalks. Wash the leaves well, then drain in a colander for about 5 minutes only. Cook the spinach in a covered pan with only the water which still adheres to its leaves. Drain well; squash out all surplus water; finely chop.

Meanwhile, wipe and finely chop the mushrooms. Heat the oil in a medium sized saucepan. Add the mushrooms and cook over a high heat for a few minutes to drive off excess moisture. Stir in the flour and cook for 1 minute. Off the heat, stir in the milk then bring to the

boil stirring all the time. Cook for 1–2 minutes; whisk in the mustard with plenty of seasoning. Off the heat, stir in the spinach; cool slightly.

Beat in the egg yolks and breadcrumbs reserving 30–45 ml (2–3 level tbsp). Whisk the egg whites until stiff but not dry, then fold into the spinach mixture. Turn into a lightly greased 1.4–1.7 litre (2½–3 pint) shallow ovenproof dish. Sprinkle over remaining crumbs. Bake alongside the potatoes at 190°C (375°F) mark 5 for about 45 minutes, or until browned and lightly set. Serve as soon as possible.

GOLDEN POTATO THATCH

These potatoes must be peeled just before cooking, as the starch from them helps to thicken and absorb the milk. Arrange quickly in the baking dish to prevent discoloration.

900 g	old potatoes	2 lb
	polyunsaturated margarine	
	1 large clove garlic	
	nutmeg	
	salt and pepper	
300 ml	milk	½ pint

Peel the potatoes, then coarsely grate through a food processor or on a hand grater. Place half in a lightly greased 1.4–1.7 litre (2½–3 pint) shallow ovenproof dish. Add the crushed garlic with a generous grating of nutmeg and plenty of seasoning. Scatter over the remaining potatoes then pour over the milk. Dot the surface with a little margarine. Place the dish on a baking sheet. Bake at 190°C (375°F) mark 5 for about 1¾ hours; or until the potatoes are tender and the top is golden brown.

WINES WITH THE FOOD

Even with the worst of winter behind us and the prospect of a glorious spring ahead, there is little fresh produce around, which is why the Grapefruit and Chick Pea Salad makes such a welcoming and refreshing starter. Sadly, finding a vinous partner for grapefruit appetisers is difficult – some wine buffs even deem it impossible. But, in fact, the strong watercress dressing is the dominant flavour of the dish and finding a wine to enhance it was not a problem. Everyone liked the vibrant, green, herbaceous flavour of the 1983 Ménétou-Salon Morogues from the Domaine Henry Pellé, owned by the local mayor. Only specialist merchants will carry this and other producers wines from the same appellation. Alternatively, you could try that well-distributed excellent racy grapefruit redolent white rioja – the Marqués de Cáceres.

The Veal and Bacon Kebabs are a much easier proposition but, once again, the orange and apricot flavours are especially strong and need a robust, full-flavoured wine. Italy provided the answer with a big, beefy 1979 Villa Antinori Chianti Classico Riserva (available from supermarkets and good wine merchants) that had sufficient fruit and bite to match the kebab and its accompaniments.

Chocolate, so the wine purists maintain, is another no-go food for wine drinkers, and I admit that a fine French Sauternes or German spätlese would probably struggle alongside the Chocolate Mousse Cake.

But Blandy's delicious pricey Ten Year Old Malmsey (from specialist merchants only) with its glorious, rich, raisiny taste should offset the chocolate-flavoured cream and yogurt mousse perfectly.

CHOCOLATE MOUSSE CAKE

The finished cake may seem a mean quantity, but it's so rich that a small wedge is all that's needed.

50 g	shelled hazelnuts	2 oz
	3 eggs, 1 egg yolk	
125 g	caster sugar	5 oz
50 g	plain flour	2 oz
5 ml	powdered gelatine	1 level tsp
100 g	plain chocolate	4 oz
50 g	polyunsaturated margarine	2 oz
142 ml	carton double cream	5 fl oz
141 g	carton natural yogurt	5 oz
	icing sugar	

Grease and base line a 20.5 cm (8 in) spring release cake tin. Toast the nuts under the grill then rub off their skins and allow to cool. Grind the nuts. Using an electric whisk, beat together 2 egg yolks and 50 g (2 oz) sugar until thick. Whisk in all but 30–45 ml (2–3 level tbsp) of the nuts. Whisk two of the egg whites until stiff but not dry. Whisk in 25 g (1 oz) sugar. Stir half the egg whites into the egg yolk mixture. Sift in the flour and fold in lightly with remaining egg white. Spoon into the prepared tin.

Bake at 180°C (350°F) mark 4 for about 20 minutes or until firm to the touch and beginning to shrink

away from the sides of the tin. Cool slightly then turn out on to a wire rack lined with sugared greaseproof paper; leave to cool. Split the cake in half and place one piece in the base of the clean spring release cake tin.

Sprinkle the gelatine over 15 ml (1 tbsp) water placed in a ramekin dish or small bowl; leave to soak for about 10 minutes. Break up the chocolate and place in a small bowl over a pan of simmering water. Heat gently, stirring occasionally, until the chocolate melts. Take off the heat and cool slightly. Meanwhile, beat the margarine with the remaining sugar. Beat in 2 egg yolks then stir in the cooled chocolate. Dissolve the gelatine by standing the dish in a pan of simmering water; then stir into the chocolate mixture.

Whisk half the cream until it just holds its shape. Stir into the mousse with half the yogurt. Fold in the remaining egg white, whisked until stiff but not dry. Spoon into the sponge lined tin and top with remaining sponge round. Refrigerate until lightly set – about 3 hours.

Ease the mousse away from the tin; loosen the tin edges then invert on to a serving dish. Dust with icing sugar if wished and decorate with reserved nuts. Refrigerate until required. Mix together the remaining yogurt and cream to serve with the Chocolate Mousse Cake cut into small wedges.

COUNTDOWN

The day before: Soak the chick peas. Prepare the kebabs and spoon over the marinade. Cover tightly and refrigerate. Prepare the Spinach and Mushroom Bake but don't add the egg whites yet; cool, cover and refrigerate. Make the Chocolate Mousse Cake; cover with cling film and refrigerate overnight.
On the morning: Cook the chick peas and complete the salad; cover tightly and refrigerate.

To Serve at 8 pm

6 pm: Preheat the oven to 190°C (375°F) mark 5. Prepare the Golden Potato Thatch and put in the oven to cook. Turn the Chocolate Mousse Cake out on to a serving plate, decorate and refrigerate.
7 pm: Take the Chick Pea Salad and spinach mixture out of the refrigerator. Chill white wine in the refrigerator.
7.15 pm: Whisk the egg whites until stiff but not dry, then complete the Spinach and Mushroom Bake. Place in the oven beside the potato dish. Start grilling the kebabs, turn and baste frequently, keep warm loosely covered in a low oven. Thicken the marinade. Check the spinach and potatoes.
8 pm: Serve the meal.

Freezer Notes

Pack and freeze the spinach and mushroom mixture without the egg whites. Thaw overnight at cool room temperature; complete as in the time plan. Leave the Chocolate Mousse Cake in its tin; do not decorate, pack and freeze. Thaw overnight in the refrigerator; take out of the tin; decorate as above. Do not freeze the Grapefruit and Chick Pea Salad, Veal and Bacon Kebabs, or the Golden Potato Thatch.

DINNER WITH A TOUCH OF STYLE

*I*f you like experimenting with cooking and with food, you'll love this menu. Although avocados can be rich, especially when puréed into a mousse, as here, our recipe is lightened with egg white and freshened with lime. The little mousses are then encased in a wafer-thin layer of smoked salmon. For the main course, we've baked crisp puff pastry cases to hold a sweetbread and veal fricassée. You'll need only a small quantity of sweet-breads, as their positive flavour soon permeates the sauce.

To finish, there's a refreshing mixture of sliced fresh pineapple topped with slivers of dried apricot soaked in orange juice and Cointreau.

AVOCADO MOUSSES WITH SMOKED SALMON

225 g	sliced smoked salmon	8 oz
15 ml	powdered gelatine	1 level tbsp
	2 small ripe avocados	
100 ml	mayonnaise	4 fl oz
60 ml	single cream	4 tbsp
15 ml	creamed horseradish	1 level tbsp
	1 egg, hard-boiled	
	juice of 2 limes	
	salt and pepper	
	1 egg white, whisked	
	watercress sprigs	
	lime wedges and Melba toast *or* Danish-type crisp rolls to accompany	

Lightly oil eight 150 ml ($\frac{1}{4}$ pint) ramekin dishes. Line the base and sides with smoked salmon. Cover with foil while preparing the mousse.

Spoon 45 ml (3 tbsp) water into a basin. Sprinkle over the gelatine and leave for about 10 minutes, or until sponge-like in texture.

Meanwhile, in a blender or food processor, purée together the avocados, the mayonnaise, cream, horseradish, hard-boiled egg, 45 ml (3 tbsp) lime juice and seasoning. When smooth, turn out into a bowl.

Dissolve the gelatine by standing the basin in a pan of simmering water. Stir in the avocado mixture, then fold in the whisked egg white. Divide between the lined ramekins, then fold excess salmon over the top. Cover each dish tightly with cling film and then refrigerate to set – about 3 hours.

To serve, turn out the mousses on to individual serving plates. Cover and leave at cool room temperature for 20–30 minutes. Garnish with the watercress sprigs.

Serve accompanied by lime wedges and Melba toast or crisp rolls.

VEAL AND SWEETBREAD PASTRIES

Lambs' sweetbreads could be used instead of calves'. Simmer initially for 2 minutes only. Leave them whole to complete the recipe.

350 g	calves' sweetbreads	12 oz
370 g	packet frozen puff pastry, thawed	13 oz
	beaten egg	
900 g	stewing veal	2 lb
300 ml	medium dry white wine	$\frac{1}{2}$ pint
	2 bay leaves	
	salt and pepper	
225 g	onion	8 oz
175 g	button mushrooms	6 oz
50 g	polyunsaturated margarine	2 oz
75 ml	flour	5 level tbsp
30 ml	single cream	2 tbsp
60 ml	fresh chopped basil	4 level tbsp
	or	
10 ml	dried basil	2 level tsp
	fresh basil leaves to garnish	

First prepare the sweetbreads. Cover them with cold water and leave to soak for 1 hour. Drain, cover with fresh water and bring to the boil. Simmer for 5 minutes, then drain and rinse. Leave in cold water until quite cold. Drain, ease off any membranes and trim fat. Place the sweetbreads between baking sheets lined with absorbent kitchen paper. Weight down lightly, then leave for 3–4 hours, or until quite firm. Slice the sweetbreads into bite-sized pieces.

Meanwhile, prepare the pastry cases. Divide the pastry in half, then roll each piece out to a 24 cm ($9\frac{1}{2}$ in) square, taking care not to stretch the pastry. Divide each piece into four squares. Using a sharp knife,

make a 1 cm (½ in) border around each square, cutting three-quarters of the way through the pastry. With the back of a knife, mark a pattern on the border.

Place the cases on two baking sheets and glaze with beaten egg. Bake at 220°C (425°F) mark 7 for about 15–18 minutes, or until well browned. Change position in the oven halfway through the cooking time to ensure even rising. Ease out the tops, then return the cases to the oven for a further 5 minutes, or until well dried out. Cool on a wire rack. Place on a baking sheet, loosely covered with foil ready for reheating.

Cut the veal into 2.5 cm (1 in) pieces, discarding skin and fat. Place in a saucepan and pour in the wine with 900 ml (1½ pints) water. Add the bay leaves and seasoning. Bring to the boil, cover and simmer for about 45 minutes, or until the veal is almost tender. Add the sliced onion and sweetbreads and simmer for a further 15 minutes, or until all the ingredients are tender.

Stir in the halved or quartered mushrooms and cook for a further 2 minutes. Strain off the seasoned cooking liquor and reserve 750 ml (1¼ pints).

Reheat the pastry cases at 180°C (350°F) mark 4 for about 10 minutes.

Melt the margarine in a large saucepan. Stir in the flour and cook for 1 minute. Mix in the reserved liquor, then bring to the boil, stirring all the time. Season to taste then stir in the meats and vegetables, discarding the bay leaves. Leave over a gentle heat, stirring occasionally, until really hot.

Mix in the cream and basil and adjust seasoning. Spoon into the pastry cases for serving. Serve the remaining sauce separately. Garnish with basil leaves.

LEAF SPINACH

This may seem an excessive amount of spinach, but it's so delicious that the recipe is well worth all the effort.

1.8 kg	fresh spinach	4 lb
40 g	butter *or* polyunsaturated margarine	1½ oz
	salt and pepper	

Pull off the spinach stalks; discard. Rinse the leaves in several changes of cold water. Drain briefly, then place in a large saucepan (or two) with only the water which adheres to the leaves.

Cover tightly and cook over a moderate heat for about 5 minutes. Drain well, squashing any excess water out of the leaves without pressing them to a pulp. Chop the spinach *roughly*.

Place the spinach, fat and seasoning in a covered saucepan. Heat gently until warm, uncover and cook over a high heat to drive off excess moisture, stirring frequently. Keep the spinach warm in a covered dish in the oven until ready to serve.

STEAMED CELERIAC

Any unused celeriac can be boiled and mashed to use another day.

1.8 kg	celeriac	4 lb
	lemon juice	
	salt and pepper	

Peel the celeriac, then, using a melon baller, scoop out celeriac balls. Immediately cover with water and lemon juice. When required, steam until tender – about 15 minutes. Keep warm in a covered dish; grind over black pepper and sprinkle with salt.

FRESH PINEAPPLE AND APRICOTS

The acidity of the pineapple is offset by the sweetness of the apricots – a perfect combination.

225 g	no-soak dried apricots	8 oz
	3 oranges	
45 ml	Cointreau	3 tbsp
	1 large pineapple	
40 g	flaked almonds	1½ oz

Snip the apricots into strips and place in a bowl. Squeeze the oranges to give 200 ml (7 fl oz) juice and strain over the apricots. Add the Cointreau and stir gently to mix. Cover tightly and refrigerate for several hours or overnight.

Meanwhile slice the pineapple into 8 pieces, about 1 cm (½ in) thick; stamp out the cores and trim away the skin. Cover the slices and refrigerate until required.

Toast the almonds until golden; when cold, store in an airtight container.

To serve, arrange the pineapple on a flat-edged platter and top with apricots and juices. Scatter over the almonds.

CHILLED CARROT AND DILL SOUP

Homemade chicken stock makes all the difference to this soup. You'll need two packets of the small supermarket packs of fresh dill for this recipe. Any leftover dill should be kept well wrapped in the refrigerator.

900 g	carrots	2 lb
	2 leeks	
1.3 litres	chicken stock	2¼ pints
45 ml	fresh chopped dill	3 level tbsp
	1 small clove garlic	
	salt and pepper	
142 ml	carton single cream	¼ pint

Pare the carrots then thinly slice. Cut the leeks into thin slices, discarding the root and any coarse green leaves; rinse well and drain.

Place the vegetables in a large saucepan with the stock, 15 ml (1 level tbsp) chopped dill, the crushed garlic and seasoning. Bring to the boil, cover and simmer until the vegetables are really tender. Cool slightly, then purée until smooth in a food processor or electric blender. Turn out into a large bowl and cool. Cover tightly and chill well in the refrigerator.

To serve, stir in 15 ml (1 level tbsp) chopped dill with the cream. Adjust seasoning and garnish with remaining chopped dill. Serve with the warmed Toasted Walnut Triangles.

California eating: clockwise from the left: Pine Nut Pilaff, Halibut with Wine and Tomatoes, Chilled Carrot and Dill Soup, Toasted Walnut Triangles and Steamed Mange Tout.

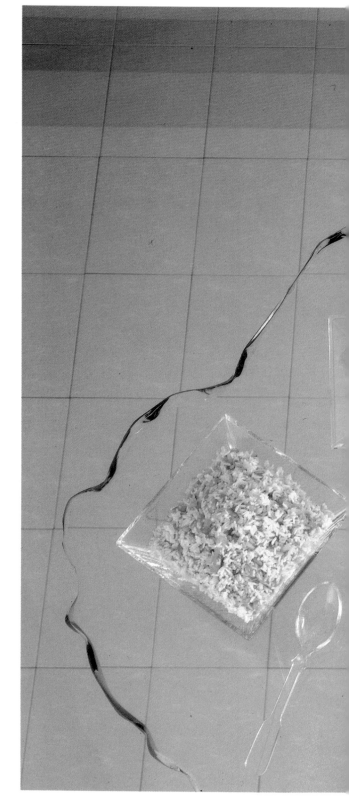

TOASTED WALNUT TRIANGLES

Make sure that the sandwiches are firmly pressed together before grilling to prevent them popping open and the contents leaking out.

75 g	walnuts	3 oz
75 g	polyunsaturated margarine	3 oz
15 ml	lemon juice	1 tbsp
	salt and pepper	
	12 small slices brown bread	

Roughly chop the walnuts then beat into the margarine with the lemon juice and seasoning. Sandwich together slices of bread with the nut mixture. Cut off the crusts, pressing each sandwich firmly together. Keep tightly covered with cling film until ready to serve.

Carefully grill the sandwiches on each side until well browned, then cut into small triangles. Serve the sandwiches just warm to accompany the Chilled Carrot and Dill Soup.

HALIBUT WITH WINE AND TOMATOES

Halibut steaks can be very large. If so, buy three steaks for six people and ease the flesh away from the bones for serving. As halibut is expensive, cod cutlets could be used instead.

450 g	ripe tomatoes	1 lb
175 g	onion	6 oz
175 g	mushrooms	6 oz
15 g	fresh root ginger	$\frac{1}{2}$ oz
45 ml	polyunsaturated oil	3 tbsp
45 ml	plain flour	3 level tbsp
150 ml	Chenin Blanc (medium dry white wine)	$\frac{1}{4}$ pint
15 ml	tomato paste	1 level tbsp
	salt and pepper	
900 g	halibut steaks (3 large or 6 small)	2 lb

Skin and roughly chop the tomatoes. Finely chop the onion; wipe and quarter the mushrooms. Peel and finely chop the ginger. Heat the oil in a frying pan; add the onion

and ginger and cook over a gentle heat for about 5 minutes; stirring occasionally. Stir in 30 ml (2 level tbsp) flour followed by the wine, tomatoes, mushrooms, tomato paste and seasoning. Bring to the boil, cook for 2 minutes; take off the heat and cool slightly.

Meanwhile, carefully ease the skin off the fish. Rinse and dry the steaks, coat with remaining flour then place in a shallow ovenproof dish which will take the fish in a single layer. Spoon over the tomato sauce.

Cover the dish tightly and place on the top shelf in the oven. Bake at 180°C (350°F) mark 4 for about 30 minutes or until the fish eases away from the bone when tested with a sharp knife. Serve with Pine Nut Pilaff and Steamed Mange Tout.

PINE NUT PILAFF

A smattering of pine nuts adds a pleasing crunchy texture to this savoury pilaff.

175 g	onion	6 oz
60 ml	polyunsaturated oil	4 tbsp
40 g	pine nuts	1½ oz
350 g	long grain white rice	12 oz
600 ml	chicken stock	1 pint
200 ml	Chenin Blanc (medium dry white wine)	7 fl oz
	salt and pepper	

Thinly slice the onion. Heat the oil in a medium-sized flame-proof casserole. Add the onion and pine nuts and cook over a high heat, stirring occasionally, until beginning to brown. Add the rice and cook, stirring for 1 minute then pour in the stock and wine. Season.

Bring the contents of the casserole to the boil. Cover tightly and place

WINES WITH THE FOOD

California really is the land of plenty – everything from the cars and scenery to the wine seems bigger, bolder and more opulent than the European equivalent. California wines can occasionally overpower English palates. The trick, as always, is to match wine to dish. However, the GH panel's tastebuds had very little trouble in selecting just what went with what.

The fresh, zingy Carrot and Dill Soup with its distinct flavour cried out for an equally racy, positive aperitif wine. We all adored Robert Mondavi's delicious strong grassy-green '83 Fumé Blanc, whose rich, full-bodied style and distinctive touch of oak made it a perfect partner. Although widely distributed, it is not the cheapest California wine available but do splash out on a bottle, for so much admired is this wine that dozens of other wineries have brought out their own Fumé Blanc versions.

On to the halibut, cooked with a good splash of a California Chenin Blanc plus tomatoes, mushrooms and ginger. As a general rule, if a recipe calls for wine it is best to serve the same wine that you have cooked with. Certainly, the North Coast Cellars', reasonably priced, lively, full, fruity Chenin Blanc was an ideal choice. (As would also be the more expensive but better distributed Mondavi Chenin Blanc.) Its peachy, slightly *pétillant* taste coped well with the ginger and fish and was inexpensive enough for even the most cost-conscious cook to use liberally in the sauce. If you are feeling flush, however, you could easily continue with the Mondavi Fumé Blanc with this course.

Finally, the rich, sweet, spicy Dried Fruit Compote demanded a similarly rich, sweet, raisiny wine and The Christian Brothers' Château La Salle is ideal.

on the lower shelf of the oven. Bake at 180°C (350°F) mark 4 for about 30 minutes or until the rice is tender and most of the stock absorbed. Adjust the seasoning.

STEAMED MANGE TOUT

Always choose small flat pods; these are the most juicy and are unlikely to be stringy.

450 g	mange tout	1 lb
	salt and pepper	
	butter *or* polyunsaturated margarine	

Top, tail and string the mange tout. Place in a metal colander or steamer, which fits over a pan of boiling salted water. Cover tightly and steam for about 3 minutes only. Mange tout are best when still a little crunchy. Place in a serving dish with seasoning and a little butter or margarine. Cover tightly and keep warm.

SPICED DRIED FRUIT COMPOTE

Little sugar is needed as the fruits add so much natural sweetness. Cinnamon sticks, available from most good supermarkets give the compote a spicy flavour without clouding the juices.

225 g	prunes	8 oz
125 g	dried apricots	4 oz
175 g	dried figs	6 oz
75 g	seedless raisins	3 oz
	1 lemon	
	6 green cardamom pods	
	mace blades	
400 ml	Chenin Blanc (medium dry white wine)	$\frac{3}{4}$ pint
25 g	soft light brown sugar	1 oz
	2 cinnamon sticks	
142 ml	carton double cream	$\frac{1}{4}$ pint
141 g	carton natural yogurt	5 oz

Place all the fruit in a large heatproof bowl with the pared lemon rind. Tie the cardamom pods and a few mace blades into a small piece

COUNTDOWN

The day before: Prepare the Chilled Carrot and Dill Soup; cool, purée. When quite cold, cover and chill overnight; keep remaining dill, covered, in the refrigerator. Skin and roughly chop the tomatoes for the halibut dish, refrigerate covered. Steep the dried fruit overnight in the wine mixture.

The morning: Prepare the sandwiches for the Toasted Walnut Triangles but don't grill yet. Cover and store in a cool place. Prepare the sauce for the fish, cool completely. Skin the fish and arrange in its cooking dish as directed. Spoon over the cold sauce, cover tightly and refrigerate. Prepare the mange tout; refrigerate in a polythene bag. Prepare Pine Nut Pilaff as far as adding the wine and seasoning, *don't* bring to the boil yet. Cover and store in a cool place. Lightly whip the cream and add the yogurt ready to accompany the compote; spoon into a serving dish; refrigerate covered.

To Serve at 8 pm

7.15 pm: Preheat the oven to 180°C (350°F) mark 4.

7.30 pm: Bring the contents of the pilaff casserole to the boil. Cover tightly and place on the lower shelf in the oven to cook. Place the fish on the top shelf of the oven.

7.45 pm: Put water on to steam for mange tout. Steam mange tout, cover and keep warm. Grill the walnut sandwiches, cut up and keep warm, loosely covered. Check the fish and rice dishes.

8 pm: Stir the cream and remaining dill into the soup; adjust seasoning and serve with the warm walnut triangles. Put the compote in the oven at 190°C (375°F) mark 5 to heat for about 25 minutes between the soup and toast starter and the main course.

Freezer Notes

Prepare the soup as far as puréeing the ingredients but don't add the cream. Pack and freeze. When required thaw overnight at cool room temperature; chill again before whisking in the cream to serve. Make the walnut sandwiches but don't grill; pack and freeze. Thaw for about 3 hours before completing as directed. Do not freeze the halibut. Freeze the compote after the initial overnight soaking of the fruits. Thaw overnight at cool room temperature then complete as above.

of muslin and place in a saucepan with the wine, 300 ml ($\frac{1}{2}$ pint) water, the sugar and cinnamon sticks. Warm gently until the sugar dissolves then bring to the boil. Pour over the fruit, stirring gently to mix. Stir occasionally while cooling, then cover and refrigerate overnight.

The next day lightly whip the cream then stir in the yogurt, cover and refrigerate. To serve the compote place all the fruit and juices in a flameproof casserole and bring to the boil. Cover tightly and bake at 190°C (375°F) mark 5 for about 25 minutes or until all the fruit is tender. Remove the muslin bag and serve hot accompanied by the cream and yogurt mixture.

SEASONAL SPRING DINNER

Menu for Six

ASPARAGUS IN A CITRUS DRESSING

LAMB NOISETTES WITH FLAGEOLET BEANS

GLAZED NEW CARROTS

BOILED NEW POTATOES

APRICOT AND WALNUT TART

With so much home produce just coming to its best in spring, there's little need to look further afield for imported 'exotic' ingredients. Tender green asparagus served just warm in a tangy dressing is followed by even more tender lamb – look out for the new season's English and serve with just the simplest of accompaniments.

To end the meal fresh apricots are baked in a walnut sponge. Use peaches for a variation. Choose three large ones, skin and cut into chunks then follow the recipe.

ASPARAGUS IN A CITRUS DRESSING

Choose slender asparagus spears (not the very thin ones known as 'sprew') as these have most flavour and make a more attractive display.

900 g	fresh asparagus	2 lb
	salt and pepper	
	2 limes	
	1 ruby grapefruit	
45 ml	polyunsaturated oil	3 tbsp

Cut the woody ends off each piece of asparagus then, using a potato peeler or small knife, scrape the stalk in order to remove any coarse spines. Rinse and drain.

Cook the asparagus in simmering salted water for about 10 minutes or until *just* tender. Drain carefully.

Meanwhile, pare the rind from one lime, then cut it into fine needle shreds, blanch in boiling water for 1 minute only, drain and reserve. Whisk together 30 ml (2 tbsp) strained lime juice, 45 ml (3 tbsp) strained grapefruit juice, the oil and seasoning.

Place the hot asparagus in the dressing and allow to marinate for about 15 minutes. Arrange the still warm asparagus on individual serving plates, spoon over a little of the dressing and garnish with the needle shreds.

LAMB NOISETTES WITH FLAGEOLET BEANS

Ask your butcher to chine the lamb for you – that is, to saw between the chine and cutlet bones.

200g	dried flageolet beans	7 oz
two 700 g	best end necks of lamb, chined	two 1½ lb
30 ml	chopped fresh parsley	2 level tbsp
	1 clove garlic	
	salt and pepper	
	fresh rosemary sprigs	

R inse the beans then place in a bowl with plenty of cold water and leave to soak in a cool place overnight. The next day, rinse the beans again and place in a saucepan with plenty of fresh water. Bring to the boil then cover and boil for about 1 hour, or until just tender. Drain, reserving the cooking liquor.

Meanwhile, place the lamb joints skin-side down on a chopping board. Then, holding the loosened chine bone in one hand, gradually ease the bone away from the 'eye' of the meat. Cut away any sinew and gristle. With the point of a small sharp knife mark through the flesh on either side of each cutlet bone, taking care not to cut through the fat and skin. Slide the knife under each bone and ease it out, scraping it clean of meat. Carefully remove any cartilage. Turn the joints over and carefully peel off the skin, trimming away any excess fat.

Place the joints flesh-side uppermost and roll up tightly from the 'eye' end. Then, using fine string, tie each one neatly at six even intervals. Chill, loosely covered, for about 30 minutes to allow the flesh to firm up. Slice each joint into six noisettes, cutting down between each piece of string.

Place three-quarters of the flageolet beans in a blender or food processor with the parsley, skinned garlic and 450 ml (¾ pint) reserved cooking liquor. Whirl until almost smooth then season to taste. Pour into a small saucepan.

Place the noisettes on a bed of rosemary sprigs on a wire rack and grill for 4–5 minutes on each side – the flesh should still be a little pink. Meanwhile, gently reheat the sauce, stirring frequently. Dip the whole beans in boiling water for 2–3 minutes to reheat then drain.

Spoon a little of the sauce on to a warmed serving plate and sit two noisettes on each plate. Garnish with the whole beans.

GLAZED NEW CARROTS

The juices bubble away as the carrots cook, to give a shiny glazed finish.

900 g	new baby carrots	2 lb
450 ml	chicken stock	¾ pint
5 ml	soft light brown sugar	1 level tsp
25 g	butter *or* polyunsaturated margarine	1 oz
	salt and pepper	
	sprigs of fresh rosemary	

T rim the carrots but leave whole; scrub the skins well. Place in a shallow saucepan with the stock, sugar, butter, seasoning and a rosemary sprig. Bring to the boil, then boil, uncovered, for about 25 minutes, or until the carrots are tender and the liquid has evaporated. Shake the pan occasionally to prevent sticking.

Adjust seasoning then garnish with a fresh rosemary sprig.

BOILED NEW POTATOES

Delicious small new potatoes are best simply boiled or steamed.

900 g	small new potatoes	2 lb
	salt and pepper	
25 g	butter *or* polyunsaturated margarine	1 oz

Wash the potatoes; scrub the skins but do not peel. Cook in boiling salted water until just tender, about 12 minutes. Drain well then toss in a little butter and season to taste.

APRICOT AND WALNUT TART

140 g	walnut halves	4½ oz
250 g	plain white flour	9 oz
150 g	polyunsaturated margarine	5 oz
	caster sugar	
	6 large firm ripe apricots	
	2 eggs	
	1 lemon	
5 ml	baking powder	1 level tsp
30 ml	apricot jam	2 level tbsp
	single cream for serving	

Reserving six walnut halves, place the remainder in a food processor and whirl until almost

WINES WITH THE FOOD

Wine hates grapefruit and is none too keen on lime either. So the asparagus first course of our dinner party menu, with its very strong lime and grapefruit dressing complete with slivers of lime peel, was definitely a challenge. The powerful dressing wiped out a lively Sauvignon, killed a lesser Muscadet and almost but not quite coped with a Sémillon blend from Chile. After such a vinous struggle, it was a relief to discover that our old GH first-course white wine standby – the classy '85 Château de la Galissonnière Muscadet de Sèvre et Maine – complemented both asparagus and dressing. The GH tasting team felt that this Muscadet's high acidity, fresh, flowery bouquet and clean, green, spritzy taste enabled it to cut through the dressing – but only just!

On to a classic French spring dish: lamb with flageolet beans cooked with garlic and rosemary. Happily, lamb has the remarkable ability to go with almost any good red wine but, as our spring lamb had such a delicate flavour, the young, delicious, light, fresh, grassy, raspberry-like '85 Caves Saint-André Chinon made the most perfect match. (Miles better than either the young claret or burgundy we also tried.) If it is a warm spring evening try serving this wine or another Chinon from the Loire chilled (to enhance its fruit) as the *servir frais* label suggests. Alternatively, you could try the rich, blackcurrant '82 Château Les Moines, Premières Côtes de Blaye, one of those up-and-coming outlying Bordeaux areas (available, like the Chinon, from good wine merchants).

To round off this spring menu we finished with a scrumptious Apricot and Walnut Tart. The crisp walnut pastry filled with a rich, soft walnut sponge and slices of fresh, ripe apricots simply cried out for a luscious and distinguished dessert wine to accompany it. The '81 Saint Croix-du-Mont Château des Coulinats (obtainable from good wine outlets), with its beautiful deep yellow-gold colour and delicious fresh peachy-pineappley taste, was exactly that.

smooth. Place 175 g (6 oz) flour in a bowl, then using a fork 'cut' in 75 g (3 oz) margarine until the mixture resembles breadcrumbs. Stir in 25 g (1 oz) ground walnuts and 5 ml (1 level tsp) sugar. Add sufficient water just to bind the pastry together, about 30–45 ml (2–3 tbsp). Knead gently then cover and chill for about 20 minutes. Roll out the pastry and use to line a 19 cm ($7\frac{1}{2}$ in) loose-based fluted flan tin. Chill for a further 20 minutes, then bake blind at 200°C (400°F) mark 6 until well dried out but not browned.

Meanwhile, peel the apricots, halve each one to remove the kernel then halve again. Cream the remaining margarine with 50 g (2 oz) sugar until light and fluffy then gradually beat in the lightly whisked eggs. Stir in the finely grated lemon rind, the remaining flour sieved with the baking powder and the remaining ground walnuts.

Spread a little of the sponge mixture over the base of the flan case, add the apricot pieces and top with the remaining mixture, smoothing the surface carefully. Arrange the reserved whole walnuts around the edge of the tart then bake at 180°C (350°F) mark 4 for about 45–50 minutes, or until just firm to the touch and golden brown. Allow the tart to cool slightly then glaze with a little warmed, sieved apricot jam. Serve warm with single cream.

COUNTDOWN

The day before: Rinse the flageolet beans then place in a bowl with plenty of cold water and leave to soak in a cool place overnight. Grind the walnuts for the Apricot and Walnut Tart. Store in an airtight container. Prepare the pastry case; bake blind until set but not browned. Allow the case to cool then store it in an airtight container.
The morning: Prepare the asparagus but do not cook yet; refrigerate in a polythene bag. Prepare the needle shreds of lime and make the citrus dressing. Store both, covered, in a cool place. Drain the beans; cook in plenty of fresh water until tender – about 1 hour. Drain again, reserving the cooking liquor. Prepare the flageolet sauce. Cool, cover and refrigerate, keeping the whole beans separate. Prepare the lamb noisettes as described, cover loosely and refrigerate. Prepare the carrots; refrigerate them in a polythene bag. Scrub the potatoes; store them in a cool place. Complete and bake the Apricot and Walnut Tart but don't glaze it yet; store in a cool place.

To Serve at 8 pm

7 pm: Cover the tart loosely with foil. Reheat at 180°C (350°F) mark 4 for 30 minutes. Cool slightly then glaze with the jam.
7.20 pm: Cook the asparagus in gently simmering salted water until the spears are *just* tender. Drain them and then put to marinate in the citrus dressing.
7.35 pm: Cook the carrots and potatoes until tender. Keep warm, covered, in a low oven.
7.45 pm: Arrange the asparagus spears on individual serving plates and garnish with lime.
7.55 pm: Grill noisettes on a bed of fresh rosemary sprigs; reheat the sauce, adding a little stock if necessary. Reheat the whole beans.
8 pm: Serve the meal.

Freezer Notes

Do not freeze either the asparagus or the noisettes of lamb with flageolet bean sauce. Bake the pastry case, cool, then freeze in a rigid container. To use, thaw at cool room temperature for about 3 hours; complete as directed.

INFORMAL VEGETARIAN SUPPER

Menu for Ten

HUMMUS WITH MINT

CRUNCHY TOPPED VEGETABLE FLANS

TOMATO AND BASIL SALAD

JACKET POTATOES WITH
SOURED CREAM DRESSING

RHUBARB AND ORANGE SUEDOISE

This vegetarian supper party could be served as a buffet in the conservatory – or even outside on warmer nights – or in a more formal setting. The array of colourful dishes makes an attractive presentation and, although there's a lot of preparation, it's all plain sailing at serving time. The crunchy vegetable flans are accompanied by a delicious tomato salad flavoured with fresh basil and jacket potatoes with an unusual topping of mango chutney blended with soured cream.

the basil and seasoning. Thinly slice the tomatoes, skinning first, if preferred. Arrange in a shallow serving dish then spoon over the dressing. Cover tightly with cling film and refrigerate for several hours to allow the flavours to marry. Take out of the refrigerator 30 minutes before serving.

JACKET POTATOES WITH SOURED CREAM DRESSING

These jacket potatoes are quite small. This way one can easily come back for seconds without feeling overwhelmed by the giant sized potatoes that are often served. Make sure they will all fit *into your oven − if not, boil them in their skins; halve for serving.*

twenty 125–175g	old potatoes	twenty 4–6 oz
90 ml	mango chutney	6 level tbsp
three 142 ml	cartons soured cream	three 5 fl oz
	salt and pepper	
	paprika pepper	

Scrub the potatoes then prick well or thread on to metal skewers. Bake at 180°C (350°F) mark 4 for about 1½ hours or until the potatoes are tender.

Meanwhile, finely chop the chutney and stir into the soured cream with seasoning to taste. Spoon into a serving dish to accompany the potatoes. Sprinkle with paprika.

— WINES WITH THE FOOD —

Just as there is no point in serving the finest fillet steak with cheap red Vin de Table, for one will definitely outshine the other, there is no point in serving a grand claret with these Crunchy Topped Vegetable Flans.

Instead the GH tasting panel opted for a glamorous aperitif glass or two of pink fizz – the delicious pretty ballet-slipper pink 1982 Crémant de Bourgogne a *méthode champenoise* burgundy bargain from supermarkets and good wine merchants. Its soft, fruity flavours, elegant livery and delightful colour make it the perfect party tipple, as does its moderate price. Having succeeded in getting everyone into a party mood, the next step is to find a wine to match the hummus with its strong olive oil and garlicky flavours. It may sound odd to serve a red wine at the first course stage but most white wines would be wiped out by this dish and everyone enjoyed the classic Greek fruity charms of the Apollo Dry Red with

the hummus, a real supermarket bargain buy.

On to the next course, a lovely crisp vegetable flan whose hazelnut pastry and crunchy green vegetables set in a cheese custard, cried out for an inexpensive rich, nutty Chardonnay to accompany it. We found the answer with an excellent '83 White Burgundy from the Buxy cooperative. It had a fresh, zappy pineapple-like Chardonnay nose plus that rich nutty white burgundy character we were looking for. You could also try the less expensive Italian '84 Lugana San Benedetto (from supermarkets and Italian specialists) whose lively, fresh grapey, sherbet-like style goes perfectly with the Tomato and Basil Salad.

The cinnamon flavoured Rhubarb and Orange Suedoise is rather too spicy for most dessert wines but our pink fizz – the '82 Crémant de Bourgogne – matches its colour and makes a delicious summer digestif.

RHUBARB AND ORANGE SUEDOISE

Tender pink rhubarb is best here as it gives a delicate colour. Meringues help to counteract the bitterness of rhubarb.

900 g	fresh rhubarb	2 lb
	2 large oranges	
2.5 ml	ground cinnamon	½ level tsp
125 g	soft light brown sugar	4 oz
	red food colouring (optional)	
30 ml	powdered gelatine	2 level tbsp
	2 egg whites	
125 g	caster sugar	4 oz
142 ml	carton double cream	¼ pint
142 ml	carton single cream	¼ pint

Wipe the rhubarb then cut into short lengths, discarding any tough ends. Place in a large saucepan. Add the grated rind of one orange. Grate the rind of the second orange straight into a clean bowl; cover tightly and refrigerate. Squeeze the juice from both oranges – there should be about 200 ml (7 fl oz) – then add to the pan. Pour in 300 ml (½ pint) water and sprinkle in the cinnamon and soft light brown sugar. Cover the pan tightly then simmer until the fruit is soft and mushy; cool slightly.

In a blender or food processor purée the pan ingredients until quite smooth – there should be about 1.4 litres (2½ pints). Purée. Pour the purée into a large bowl; add a little food colouring if wished. Spoon 90 ml (6 tbsp) water into a small bowl then sprinkle over the gelatine. Leave to stand for about 10 minutes, or until sponge-like in texture. Stand the basin in a pan of simmering water until the gelatine mixture is liquid and quite clear. Stir into the rhubarb. Ladle the mixture into 10 individual serving dishes, preferably glass. Cover and refrigerate to set, preferably overnight.

Meanwhile prepare small meringues. Whisk the egg whites until stiff but not dry. Whisk in 30 ml (2 level tbsp) caster sugar until the mixture returns to its former stiff-

ness. Fold in remaining caster sugar. Spoon or pipe the mixture into small meringue shapes on baking sheets lined with non-stick paper. (There should be about 50 meringues.) Dry out in the oven set at 100°C (200°F) mark low for about 1½ hours. Cool on a wire rack then store in an airtight container.

To serve the suedoise, lightly whip the creams until they hold their shape then fold in the reserved orange rind, keeping a little for decoration. Spoon into the individual serving dishes and top with meringues. Decorate with orange rind.

COUNTDOWN

Two days ahead: Soak the chick peas overnight. Make the meringues. Cool then store in an airtight container.

The day before: Make the hummus, cover tightly and refrigerate. Prepare the pastry cases and bake blind, don't fill yet. When cold, cover tightly and store in a cool place. Cook the rhubarb and make the suedoise, refrigerate tightly covered.

The morning: Wrap pitta bread in foil ready to reheat. Prepare, blanch and sauté the vegetables for the flans. Do not add to the flan yet; cover, store in a cool place. Prepare the cheese custard mixture and the nut topping. Keep both covered separately in a cool place. Make the Tomato and Basil Salad; cover and store in a cool place. Scrub the potatoes ready to cook, don't prick them yet. Make the chutney and soured cream dressing and refrigerate covered. Whip the creams together, add the orange rind and leave in the refrigerator covered.

To Serve at 8 pm

About 6.15 pm: Preheat the oven to 180°C (350°F) mark 4. Prick the potatoes and place in the oven. Fill the flan cases and place in the oven to cook.

7.30 pm: Take the hummus and Tomato and Basil Salad out of the refrigerator.

7.45 pm: Check the flans. Remove from oven once cooked. Just before serving, pop the pitta bread, wrapped in silver foil, into the oven to warm through.

8 pm: Serve the meal. Don't forget the soured cream dressing. Complete the Rhubarb and Orange Suedoise just before serving.

Freezer Notes

Do not freeze the hummus; it becomes granular on thawing. Bake the pastry cases blind, cool, pack in rigid containers and freeze. Spoon the filling into the frozen flan cases and bake as before. Do not freeze the Rhubarb and Orange Suedoise.

DINNER WITH A CHINESE TOUCH

This is a meal which needs an informal setting. Chinese food inevitably means last-minute cooking, but if you serve it in the kitchen or close by, you can stir-fry the beef and vegetable recipes in between courses without neglecting your guests. Chinese cuisine is not renowned for its desserts, so we suggest serving a plate of exotic fruits and ending the meal with jasmine tea.

HOT AND SOUR PRAWN SOUP

Don't be tempted to use sesame oil alone – its aromatic, nutty flavour will overpower the other ingredients.

125 g	peeled prawns	4 oz
	1 lemon	
45 ml	dry sherry	3 tbsp
50 g	onion	2 oz
50 g	*small* button mushrooms	2 oz
15 ml	polyunsaturated oil	1 tbsp
10 ml	white flour	2 level tsp
30 ml	dark soy sauce	2 tbsp
750 ml	chicken stock	1¼ pints
5 ml	sesame oil	1 tsp
	salt and pepper	
	coriander leaves to garnish	

Place the prawns in a bowl; add the finely grated rind of the lemon and 30 ml (2 tbsp) strained juice. Stir in the sherry, cover and marinate for about 1 hour. Meanwhile, thinly slice the onion; wipe and thinly slice the mushrooms.

Heat the polyunsaturated oil in a saucepan, stir in the onion and mushrooms and cook, stirring, for 1–2 minutes. Mix in the flour and cook for a further minute. Add the soy sauce and stock, bring to the boil, reduce heat then cover and simmer for about 10 minutes. Mix in the prawns and marinade, cover and simmer for a further 5 minutes. Stir in the sesame oil and season to taste. Garnish with coriander leaves.

CRISPY ROAST DUCKLING

Peking duck, a firm favourite in Chinese restaurants, is difficult to re-create at home. Our variation is much simpler.

two 225 g	duckling breast fillets	two 8 oz
45 ml	runny honey	3 tbsp
	hoisin barbecue sauce	
5 ml	Chinese 5-spice powder	1 level tsp
	salt and pepper	
	1 bunch spring onions	
	½ cucumber	
1 quantity of pancakes (see next recipe)		

Wipe the duckling fillets then, with a sharp knife, slash the skin. Place the fillets, skin-side uppermost, in a shallow-edged stainless dish. Mix the honey, 15 ml (1 level tbsp) hoisin sauce, the 5-spice powder and seasoning. Pour over the duck, cover and refrigerate for at least 3 hours, turning once.

Meanwhile, prepare the spring onion brushes. Trim the onions, discarding the coarse green part. Cut the remainder into 5 cm (2 in) lengths and, using a small, sharp knife, cut both ends into strips, leaving the centre part intact. Place in a bowl of iced water and refrigerate for at least 2 hours, or until the ends begin to curl up. To make the cucumber sticks, cut the cucumber into thin diagonal slices, then into matchstick-size pieces. Cover and refrigerate.

Lift the duckling fillets on to a wire rack, placed over a foil-lined roasting tin, and spoon on one-third of the marinade. Bake at 200°C (400°F) mark 6 for about 25–30 minutes, basting frequently with the remaining marinade. When cooked, the juices of the duckling should run clear when the skin is pierced with a fine skewer.

Thinly slice the duckling and garnish with the spring onion brushes. To serve, each person spreads hoisin sauce over a pancake, adds slices of duckling and cucumber sticks and rolls it up.

PANCAKES

We experimented with various batters and doughs to try and achieve pancakes similar to those served in Chinese restaurants but weren't happy with the results. Instead we suggest making the traditional pancakes below. Alternatively, you can buy them from Chinese supermarkets.

125 g	plain white flour	4 oz
	1 egg	
200 ml	milk	7 fl oz
	salt and pepper	
	polyunsaturated oil	

Place the flour, egg, milk and seasoning in a blender or food processor with 15 ml (1 tbsp) oil and 75 ml (3 fl oz) water. Whirl until just smooth, then leave to stand for about 30 minutes.

Heat a small, well-seasoned frying pan until hot then brush with as little oil as possible. Ladle a small amount of batter into the pan, swirling it around the surface. Cook over a high heat until golden brown then flip over and cook the underside. Turn out on to a cooling rack lined with a tea towel. Cover. Cook the remaining pancakes similarly (adding more oil to the pan if necessary), layering them between sheets of non-stick paper. Cool and overwrap in foil ready to reheat.

When required, reheat on the lower shelf in an oven set at 200°C (400°F) mark 6 for about 10 minutes, or until thoroughly hot. Serve as soon as possible with the crispy roast duckling.

STIR-FRIED FILLET STEAK WITH MANGO

Wear rubber gloves when preparing the chillies as they contain a substance which can burn the skin. We've suggested 2–3 chillies – their strength varies, so use sparingly.

350 g	fillet steak	12 oz
15–25 g	piece fresh root ginger	½–1 oz
	2–3 medium-sized fresh green chillies	
30 ml	dark soy sauce	2 tbsp
60 ml	polyunsaturated oil	4 tbsp
	1 clove garlic	
	salt and pepper	
	2 medium-sized firm ripe mangoes	
30 ml	beef stock	2 tbsp

Shred the steak into wafer-thin slices, cutting with the grain of the meat. Peel and finely chop the ginger. Halve the chillies; carefully scoop out the seeds and discard. Finely chop the flesh. Place the beef, ginger and chillies into a bowl and stir in the soy sauce, half the oil, and the crushed garlic and seasoning. Cover and refrigerate for at least 4 hours.

Meanwhile, cut thick slices of mango flesh off either side of the stone then thinly slice. Trim the skin, cover and refrigerate until required.

Heat the remaining oil in a wok or large frying pan. Add the beef to the wok or pan and cook, stirring,

WINES WITH THE FOOD

No one likes to admit defeat, but I confess that the GH cooks very nearly had me doing just that. This Chinese-style dinner for four presents such a mine-field of fierce flavours that, no matter how powerful the wines I presented as possible partners, all – well, nearly all – failed dismally.

The first Chinese dish was a refreshing bowl of Hot and Sour Prawn Soup, which tasted strongly of smoked sesame oil, and its garnish of coriander leaves. My vinous attempts with this starter included a fruity Italian Pinot Blanc and an elegant but full-bodied Chardonnay, also from Italy. Neither worked and in the end we all felt that the only possible accompaniment to the soup was a fine, dry, pungent, salty Manzanilla sherry, a little of which can be used in the soup, and also as an aperitif beforehand. The top supermarkets' Pale Dry Manzanillas often make elegant, yeasty examples, but better still is the fine, nutty Barbadillo Manzanilla.

On to the two main course dishes: the classic Chinese Crispy Roast Duckling served with strong spring onions and a very spicy hoisin sauce, and the fillet steak cooked with very powerful fresh root ginger and juicy mangoes. Given the strength of these flavours, it was perhaps not surprising that the two Rhône reds we tasted wilted with the food. Somewhat miraculously, the '81 Lagrein Dunkel Riserva from J Tiefenbrunner in Italy did work (from specialist merchants only). I enjoyed the deep purple colour and big, burnt, almost inky style of this wine but the rest of the panel was not so keen. If you feel your guests might not necessarily like this style of wine either, then have ample supplies of hot jasmine tea or cold lager ready to slake their thirsts. Both these beverages go with most Chinese dishes and can easily be drunk throughout the meal.

Finally, one of the lighter, luscious, flowery Moscatels de Valencia made an ideal partner for the exotic fresh fruit dessert.

over a high heat for 1–2 minutes. Stir in the stock and cook for a further 3–4 minutes. Stir in the mango. Adjust the seasoning. Serve.

CABBAGE AND BEAN SPROUTS

Cooking the vegetables over a high heat for the minimum of time helps to retain their flavour and texture.

275 g	spring greens *or* green cabbage	10 oz
	1 bunch spring onions	
30 ml	polyunsaturated oil	2 tbsp
20 ml	dark soy sauce	4 tsp
175 g	fresh bean sprouts	6 oz
	salt and pepper	

Finely shred the spring greens or cabbage. Wash well and pat dry. Trim the onions; cut into 2.5 cm (1 in) diagonal slices. Heat the oil in a wok or large frying pan, add the spring greens and onions and cook, stirring, over a high heat for 1–2 minutes. Mix in the soy sauce and bean sprouts and cook for a further minute. Adjust seasoning and serve.

BOILED THREAD NOODLES

These delicious noodles require only the minimum amount of cooking. Stir in the sesame oil for serving.

	salt and pepper	
250 g	packet thread egg noodles	8.8 oz
5 ml	sesame oil	1 tsp

Bring a large pan of salted water to the boil. Add the noodles and boil, uncovered, for 3–4 minutes or until *just* cooked. Return to the saucepan, stir in the oil and season to taste.

COUNTDOWN

The day before: Marinate the prawns in the lemon juice and sherry then complete the soup as directed. Cool, cover and refrigerate. Prepare the pancakes, overwrap with foil and refrigerate.
The morning: Marinate the duckling fillets as directed, cover and refrigerate, turning once. Prepare the spring onion brushes, place in iced water and refrigerate. Prepare the cucumber sticks and refrigerate in a polythene bag. Marinate the fillet steak as directed, cover and refrigerate. Slice the mango, cover and refrigerate. Shred the spring greens or cabbage then wash and pat dry. Refrigerate in a polythene bag. Slice the spring onions and refrigerate covered.

TO SERVE AT 8 PM

7.15 pm: Preheat the oven to 200°C (400°F) mark 6.
7.25 pm: Cook the duckling on a wire rack, placed over a foil-lined roasting tin; baste frequently. Arrange a selection of fresh fruits on a plate.
7.45 pm: Assemble all the ingredients for the Stir-fried Fillet Steak with Mango and the Cabbage and Bean Sprouts. Reheat the pancakes on the bottom shelf of the oven. Bring a large saucepan of water to the boil, ready for the noodles.
7.55 pm: Reheat the soup; remember to garnish with the coriander leaves just before serving.
8 pm: Serve the soup then the duckling. Stir-fry the beef with mango, the cabbage and bean sprouts and cook the noodles just before serving.

FREEZER NOTES

Make the pancakes, interleave with nonstick paper and overwrap with foil. Freeze. Thaw for 3–4 hours then reheat as directed.

SUMMER BUFFET

Menu for Twelve

SEAFOOD PASTRIES

SPICED CHICKEN TERRINES
WITH HERBED MAYONNAISE

CUCUMBER MOUSSE

POTATO AND CELERY SALAD

TOSSED GREEN SALAD

ASSORTED CHEESES

CHOCOLATE TORTES

FRESH FRUIT BOWL

*S*ummer is the perfect time to throw open the doors and call up friends you haven't seen for some time. The easiest way to entertain a crowd of more than six is to serve a buffet meal planned around large plates of interestingly shaped, individual bites as well as a variety of rather more substantial dishes. If possible include one hot dish, just in case the weather is less than perfect. Swell the summer feast further with a simple selection of cheeses and crispbreads.

The menu is planned so that most of the dishes can be made at least one or two days in advance, cutting out that last-minute panic.

SEAFOOD PASTRIES

You could use different types of fish and shellfish for the filling but fresh salmon and prawns make a lovely flavour combination.

The authentic taste of summer; clockwise from the left: Spiced Chicken Terrines, Herbed Mayonnaise, Tossed Green Salad, Potato and Celery Salad, Cucumber Mousse and Seafood Pastries.

200 g	filo pastry (strudel leaves)	7 oz
50 g	unsalted butter	2 oz
50 g	polyunsaturated margarine	2 oz
400 g	filleted salmon	14 oz
175 g	fresh peeled prawns	6 oz
78 g	packet full-fat soft cheese with garlic and herbs	$2\frac{1}{4}$ oz
	black pepper	

Cut the filo pastry into 15 cm (6 in) squares, reserving any trimmings. Stack the squares together in a pile and cover.

Take one square and lightly brush both sides with the butter and margarine melted together. Put a small piece of pastry trimming into the centre of the square to reinforce the base of the pastry.

Skin the salmon, cut into 1 cm ($\frac{1}{2}$ in) cubes and arrange 2–3 cubes of fish in the middle of the pastry. Top with 2–3 prawns and dot with a small spoonful of cheese. Season with black pepper.

Gather the edges of the pastry into a bundle, pressing firmly together. Transfer them to a greased baking tray. Repeat the buttering, filling and shaping process until all the fish is used.

Bake the bundles at 180°C (350°F) mark 4 for 15–20 minutes, or until the pastry is crisp and golden. Serve warm or cold.

MAKES ABOUT 36

SPICED CHICKEN TERRINES WITH HERBED MAYONNAISE

Layers of chicken and spinach mixed with a little rice, walnuts, apricots and spices make a moist and attractive main-course combination.

175 g	brown rice	6 oz
	salt and pepper	
150 g	dried apricots, soaked	5 oz
two 300 g	packets frozen leaf spinach	two 11 oz
100 g	walnut pieces	4 oz
15 ml	ground cumin	1 level tbsp
10 ml	ground coriander	2 level tbsp
	1 large egg, beaten	
each 100 g	10–12 chicken breast fillets	each 4 oz
	polyunsaturated oil	
24 g	packet aspic jelly	0.85 oz
	watercress to garnish	
300 ml	thick mayonnaise	$\frac{1}{2}$ pint
	chopped fresh herbs of your choice	

Cook the brown rice in boiling salted water until tender – about 30 minutes; drain. Cut the apricots into slivers; thaw the spinach and drain well, pressing out excess moisture; roughly chop the walnuts. Mix all these together with the spices, seasoning and egg.

Trim the chicken of any fat or sinew and sear 3–4 pieces at a time in a very hot, lightly oiled frying pan. When the chicken is golden brown on both sides, but not cooked through, remove the pieces and set aside. Repeat with the rest. Allow to cool.

Cut through each chicken breast (slightly on the diagonal) making 3–4 fairly thick slices. Arrange half the chicken in the base of two 11×23 cm ($4\frac{1}{2} \times 9$ in) non-stick loaf tins, browned flesh facing downwards. Spoon over the rice mixture. Cover with the rest of the chicken fried-side up and put a piece of foil over the top. Stand the tins in a dish half filled with warm water and bake at 180°C (350°F) mark 4 for about 1 hour 20 minutes, or until the chicken feels firm when pressed. Leave to cool in the tins. When cold, refrigerate for 2–3 hours only. Turn out of the tins, wash the tins and replace the terrines.

Make up the packet of aspic following manufacturer's instructions. Cool, then pour over the two terrines. Return to the refrigerator to set – about 2 hours. Turn out and slice. Garnish and serve with mayonnaise mixed with herbs.

CUCUMBER MOUSSE

The finished mousse looks small for 12 people but it's surprising how far it goes.

25 ml	gelatine	5 level tsp
90 ml	mayonnaise	6 level tbsp
60 ml	thick cream *or* curd cheese	4 level tbsp
15 ml	sugar	1 level tbsp
5 ml	salt	1 level tsp
45 ml	lemon juice	3 tbsp
15 ml	white wine vinegar	1 tbsp
	2 small cucumbers, grated	
	white pepper	

Sprinkle the gelatine over 75 ml (5 tbsp) water in a heatproof basin and leave to soak for 10 minutes. Dissolve by standing the basin in a pan of simmering water.

Whisk together the mayonnaise and cream or cheese with the sugar, salt, lemon juice, vinegar and 400 ml (14 fl oz) water; stir in the dissolved gelatine. Leave until just beginning to set then fold in 250 ml (8 fl oz) grated cucumber and check the seasoning. Turn into a 900 ml (1½ pint) soufflé dish and chill until set. Turn out and garnish with cucumber slices.

POTATO AND CELERY SALAD

The potatoes look better peeled but if time is short leave the skins on.

1.4 kg	small new potatoes	3 lb
	salt and pepper	
100 g	streaky bacon	4 oz
60 ml	lemon juice	4 tbsp
120 ml	chicken stock	4 fl oz
30 ml	polyunsaturated oil	2 tbsp
15 ml	white wine vinegar	1 tbsp
	pinch sugar	
75 ml	thinly sliced spring onions	5 level tbsp
	1 stick celery	
	paprika pepper	

Boil the unpeeled potatoes until tender. Drain; peel as soon as they are cool enough to handle. Place them in a heated bowl; season.

Meanwhile, cut the bacon into strips and fry until crispy. Drain and set aside. Whisk the lemon juice, stock, oil, vinegar, sugar and onions together. Stir in the celery cut into strips and pour the mixture over the hot potatoes. Sprinkle with bacon and paprika. Allow to cool for about 30 minutes before serving.

CHOCOLATE TORTES

The good news about this chocoholic delight is that, with whipped topping and yogurt instead of cream, the end result is far lower in calories yet still deliciously rich in texture.

225 g	plain chocolate	8 oz
two 150 g	cartons black cherry yogurt	two 5.2 oz
284 ml	carton Greek yogurt	10 fl oz
284ml	carton double cream	10 fl oz
60 ml	toasted flaked almonds	4 level tbsp
90 ml	brandy	6 tbsp
30 ml	milk	2 tbsp
	36 sponge finger biscuits	
284 ml	carton double *or* whipping cream	10 fl oz
	chocolate curls *or* chocolate flake bars and strawberries to decorate	

Break up the chocolate and melt in a large bowl over hot water. Cool slightly and whisk in the cherry and the Greek yogurt. Whisk the double cream until stiff then fold into the mixture. Fold in the nuts.

Mix the brandy and milk in a shallow dish and dip half the sponge fingers, one at a time, into this mixture. Arrange across the base of two 11×23 cm $(4\frac{1}{2} \times 9$ in) loaf tins lined with cling film overhanging at the sides (trim the biscuits if necessary). Spoon over the chocolate mixture. Dip the remaining biscuits in the brandy and milk and arrange on top. Wrap the cling film over the cakes to shape into an oblong. Freeze until firm – about 3 hours.

Unwrap the cling film and turn the cakes out on to plates or trays. Spread the top lightly with a little of the whipping cream, whipped, and use the rest to pipe swirls down both long top edges. Fill the centre with chocolate curls or splinters of chocolate flake. Serve, decorated with strawberries.

WINES WITH THE FOOD

This summer buffet menu is an enchanting combination of delicious fresh summer flavours. The Seafood Pastries in particular are delectable, dainty-looking little parcels of salmon and prawn spiked with garlic and herbs. The GH tasting panel much enjoyed an Alsace wine with this dish – the '84 Auxerrois from the delightfully named Rolly-Gassmann. The Auxerrois grape is thought by some Alsace winemakers to be a distant relative of the Chardonnay and its pale greeny-gold colour and lovely, floral, summery bouquet and palate certainly impressed the GH tasters. Given the lively, invigorating, *pétillant* nature of the wine, it would also make a good aperitif (specialist wine merchants only).

On to the moreish Spiced Chicken Terrines, whose flavourings of apricots and walnuts, plus cumin and coriander, accompanied by a light, tangy Cucumber Mousse and flavoursome Potato and Celery Salad, merited a more full-flavoured wine (although a few of us thought that the Alsace wine was entirely capable of matching this dish). The Loire's splendid '85 Pouilly Blanc Fumé, Les Griottes from Michel Bailly, (obtainable from supermarkets and wine merchants), one of the finest producers in Pouilly, with its young, crisp, verdant taste of gooseberries and nettles, was an excellent choice and also went well with the Seafood Pastries. For those who like to drink red wines, warm weather or no, the GH choice is the '83 Château Thieuley whose lovely, ripe, raspberry-redcurranty flavour would be delicious served slightly chilled with the terrines (available from good wine merchants). It would also make an excellent partner for any summer cheeseboard.

For dessert, glorious, tempting Chocolate Tortes. Strictly speaking, chocolate hates wine but as this summer buffet is likely to be lingered over, give everyone a chance to eat a piece of fresh fruit to clear their palates, and then serve a peachy-pineappley half bottle of Sauternes – the '84 Château Guiteronde du Hayot (from supermarkets and wine merchants).

COUNTDOWN

A week ahead: make Chocolate Tortes and freeze.
2–3 days before: make the vinaigrette dressing for the green salad.
The day before: Make but don't bake Seafood Pastries; cover and refrigerate. Make Chicken Terrines. Chop the herbs for the mayonnaise; make Cucumber Mousse; refrigerate both covered. Wash the salad ingredients; scrub potatoes. Prepare dressing for potatoes; fry bacon and store in a cool place.

TO SERVE AT 8 PM

5 pm: Assemble a bowl of fruit.
About 6.30 pm: Bake Seafood Pastries; slice Chicken Terrines; mix mayonnaise with herbs; make potato salad; mix green salad but don't dress yet. Turn out and decorate Cucumber Mousse. Unwrap cheeses.
7 pm: Thaw Chocolate Tortes at cool room temperature.
7.55 pm: Pour dressing over green salad.
8 pm: Serve the meal.

FREEZER NOTES

Pack and freeze the Seafood Pastries before baking – *use fresh prawns only*. Thaw for 1½ hours before baking. Freeze Chocolate Tortes as directed.

INFORMAL SUMMER SUPPER

*S*imple to prepare yet impressive to the eye, this dinner for four is ideal for informal occasions. Because much is prepared ahead last minute panic is considerably reduced.

It is well worth seeking out butterfly lamb chops, which, because they are cut from across the carcass, are attractive and meaty. Order these double chops in advance. Alternatively serve two single chops per person. The courgettes with carrots provide a colourful accompaniment for the chops.

LEMON CHEESE FLAN

A tangy cheese mixture in a rich short-crust pastry case.

175 g	plain white flour	6 oz
75 g	polyunsaturated margarine	3 oz
20 ml	caster sugar	4 level tsp
	1 egg	
225 g	cottage cheese	8 oz
150 g	carton natural yogurt	5 oz
	1 lemon	
5 ml	powdered gelatine	1 level tsp

Place the flour in a bowl, then using a fork 'cut' in the margarine. Stir in 5 ml (1 level tsp) sugar and the egg yolk. Add sufficient water to bind to a soft dough.

Roll out the pastry on a lightly floured surface then use to line a 20.5 cm (8 in) fluted flan ring placed on a baking sheet. Chill for about 20 minutes then bake blind at 200°C (400°F) mark 6 until set and lightly browned. Cool.

Meanwhile, sieve the cottage cheese into a bowl, beat in the yogurt and grated lemon rind. Place 45 ml (3 tbsp) water in a small bowl and sprinkle over the gelatine. Allow to stand for about 10 minutes or until sponge-like in texture. Dissolve the gelatine by standing the bowl in a pan of simmering water. When liquid and clear stir into the cheese mixture with the remaining sugar. Lightly whisk the egg white until stiff, not dry, then fold into the mixture.

Pour the cheese mixture into the cooled flan case and refrigerate until set, about 3 hours. Cover and chill until required. Remove from the refrigerator about 30 minutes before serving with the Red Fruit Salad.

RED FRUIT SALAD

Add a little more sugar to the fruit salad if preferred – it is quite tart.

125 g	redcurrants	4 oz
125 g	blackcurrants	4 oz
60 ml	unsweetened apple juice	4 tbsp
50 g	granulated sugar	2 oz
125 g	raspberries	4 oz
225 g	strawberries	8 oz

Top and tail the redcurrants and blackcurrants. Place in a small saucepan with the apple juice. Cover and simmer until the fruits pop and begin to soften. Immediately stir in the sugar until dissolved; pour out into a bowl and cool.

Wipe the raspberries, wash and hull the strawberries, slice any that are large. Stir into the cold blackcurrants and redcurrants. Cover and refrigerate for at least 3 hours. Serve with the Lemon Cheese Flan.

COUNTDOWN

The day before: Trim and prepare the butterfly chops. Place in a shallow dish (non-metallic) with the marinade. Cover and refrigerate overnight, turning once. Bake the flan case, cool then store in an airtight container.

On the morning: Prepare the port dressing, add the prawns, cover and refrigerate. Wash the lamb's lettuce, dry thoroughly, refrigerate in a polythene bag. Thinly slice the fennel, spoon over the lemon juice, cover and refrigerate. Prepare the stuffing for the chops, but do not use it yet. Prepare the carrots and courgettes; place in the fridge in separate polythene bags. Complete the flan, cover and leave to set in the refrigerator. Prepare the Red Fruit Salad, cover and refrigerate.

To Serve at 8 pm

6.45 pm: Preheat the oven to 180°C (350°F) mark 4.

7 pm: Remove the chops from the marinade, add the stuffing and secure well with cocktail sticks. Complete as directed.

About 7.15 pm: Arrange the lamb's lettuce, fennel and prawns on individual serving plates. Spoon over the dressing. Cook the potatoes, keep warm covered in a low oven. Blanch the carrots, complete as directed. Check the

lamb. Transfer to a warmed serving dish, cover and keep warm in a low oven. Skim and thicken the juices.

About 8 pm: Remove the flan and fruit salad from the refrigerator. Serve the meal.

FREEZER NOTES

Do not freeze the Prawns in Port Dressing. Cook the Mustard Lamb Chops for 30 minutes only. Cool, pack and freeze before thickening. Thaw overnight at cool room temperature. Return to the casserole dish, bring the juices to the boil, cover and reheat at 180°C (350°F) mark 4 for about 20 minutes or until hot and thoroughly tender. Complete as above. Bake the flan case, cook, pack and freeze in a rigid container. Thaw for about 3 hours; complete as directed.

A Light Summer Special

Here we've put together an easy-to-prepare menu which makes the best use of seasonal fare. Avocado and raspberry, one rich and creamy, the other sharp and fresh, combine perfectly in the starter.

Fresh tarragon is such a treat it's worth seeking out to enliven the chicken dish. If the tarragon sprigs appear withered pour a little water into a narrow jug or jar and place the base stems only in the water. Cover completely the top of the jar and the tarragon with a polythene bag and leave in the fridge for an hour or so. Unless the tarragon was dried beyond redemption you'll find it will miraculously recover and become a vibrant herb again.

Avocado with Raspberry Vinegar

The fruity sharpness of the raspberries perfectly offsets the richness of the avocados.

125 g	fresh raspberries	4 oz
75 ml	white wine vinegar	5 tbsp
45 ml	olive oil	3 tbsp
90 ml	polyunsaturated oil	6 tbsp
	salt and pepper	
	2 firm, ripe avocados	
	small head radicchio	

Pick over the raspberries and place half in a small bowl. Heat the vinegar until beginning to bubble then pour over the raspberries in the bowl. Leave to steep for at least 1 hour. Strain off, pressing the fruit *gently* to extract all juices but not the pulp. Reserve the vinegar, whisk together with the oils and seasoning.

Carefully halve each avocado and twist out the stone. Peel away the skin then slice the flesh straight into the dressing. Stir gently until the avocado is completely covered in

dressing. Cover tightly and refrigerate for about 2 hours. Meanwhile separate the radicchio leaves, rinse and drain. Dry on kitchen paper, then refrigerate in a polythene bag.

To serve, place a few radicchio leaves on individual plates. Spoon on the avocado mixture and garnish with the remaining fresh raspberries.

CHICKEN WITH TARRAGON

Always measure dried herbs with care as they can be pungent and an overdose will ruin the subtle flavour of the dish.

700 g	6 chicken breast fillets, total weight	1½ lb
	1 small bunch spring onions	
45 ml	flour	3 level tbsp
	1 lemon	
15 ml	fresh chopped tarragon	1 level tbsp
	or	
5 ml	dried tarragon	1 level tsp
	salt and pepper	
30 ml	polyunsaturated oil	2 tbsp
15 g	butter	½ oz
450 ml	chicken stock	¾ pint
15 ml	single cream	1 tbsp
(buy a 142 ml (¼ pint) carton and serve the remainder with the Peach and Pecan Crisps)		
	fresh tarragon sprigs to garnish	

If necessary skin the fillets then place two at a time between sheets of cling film. Bat out until very thin; cut each fillet in half. Trim the spring onions discarding the coarse dark green leaves; thinly slice. Mix the flour with the finely grated lemon rind, the herbs and seasoning. Dip the chicken into the seasoned flour.

Heat the oil and butter in a large sauté pan. Brown the chicken pieces a few at a time; adding a little more oil if necessary. Take out of the pan. Add the onion and stir-fry for 1 minute. Mix in any remaining flour with the stock, 15 ml (1 tbsp) lemon juice and seasoning. Bring to the boil then replace the chicken.

Cover the pan tightly and simmer gently for 10–15 minutes or until the chicken is tender. Carefully skim any fat from the juices then remove from the heat; adjust seasoning and stir in the cream.

Garnish with a few fresh tarragon sprigs just before serving.

CREAMED BROCCOLI

This puréed broccoli is lightly set in a ring mould then sliced for serving. Leave it for 10 minutes to firm up before turning out.

450 g	broccoli	1 lb
100 g	onion	4 oz
	1 clove garlic	
300 ml	light stock or water	½ pint
	salt and pepper	
75 g	low-fat soft cheese	3 oz
	3 eggs	
	fresh brown breadcrumbs	
	polyunsaturated margarine	

Thinly slice the broccoli stalks and divide the heads into small florets. Wash together and drain well. Slice the onion, skin the garlic and cut into fine strips.

Place the broccoli, onion, and garlic in a saucepan with the stock or water and seasoning. Bring to the boil, cover and simmer gently until the vegetables are quite tender, about 20–30 minutes. Cool slightly then purée with the cheese in an electric blender or food processor until almost smooth. Turn out into a bowl then whisk in the eggs and 50 g (2 oz) breadcrumbs. Adjust the seasoning.

Chicken with Tarragon, Creamed Broccoli and New Potatoes

Lightly grease a 1.1 litre (2 pint) ring mould and sprinkle with bread-crumbs. Spoon in the broccoli mixture then cover with greased foil. Stand the tin in a roasting tin half filled with water.

Bake at 180°C (350°F) mark 4 for about 1 hour, or until just firm to the touch. Leave to firm up for about 10 minutes then loosen from the edges of the tin. Invert on to a serving plate.

BAKED NEW POTATOES

Golden new potatoes laced with garlic.

700 g	small new potatoes	1½ lb
45 ml	polyunsaturated oil	3 tbsp
	salt and pepper	
	1 large clove garlic	

Scrub the potatoes; don't peel. Halve the larger potatoes, leave the remainder whole then lightly brown in the oil in a medium-sized flameproof casserole. Season well and add the crushed garlic. Cover

WINES WITH THE FOOD

With fruit, vegetables and flowers in full bloom, summer is an ideal time for entertaining. Any meal highlighting the pick of the summer's crop – as this dinner party does – is bound to be a delicious treat.

Conservative wine buffs are keen on claiming that certain strong spices and relishes are death for any decent wine. Vinegar is one of them. So it was with a certain foolhardiness that I put forward a choice of white wines to match the first course of Avocado with Raspberry Vinegar. One, a dry white Graves, the '84 Château Pessan, passed the test, chiefly, I suspect, because apart from that classic, green, almost dusty Sémillon grape character, this '84 had a very high acidity that enabled its flavours to sing out over the raspberry vinegar. Other dry white Graves from vintages such as '85 and '86 might also be worth a try.

If you feel this combination of invigorating acidity would be too much, try instead a glass of Raspberry Fizz. Before your guests arrive, simply purée a small quantity of fresh raspberries by rubbing them through a nylon sieve, or process them briefly then sieve; adding a sugar syrup to taste. Having chilled a bottle of the deliciously inexpensive and widely obtainable crisp, clean and fruity G F Cavalier Brut, all you need to do is pour a dollop of the raspberry purée into the bottom of a glass and top up with the sparkling wine to make a refreshingly fizzy pink summer drink.

The main course of chicken breasts, prepared with a creamy French tarragon sauce, accompanied by new potatoes with garlic, called for another positive white wine. The lively, grassy-green nettly '84 Sauvignon St Bris from Jean Deligny coped admirably as no doubt would other vintages from the same Burgundy appellation.

Our pudding wine, an '83 Monbazillac from the Unidor St Laurent des Vignes cooperative, similarly modestly priced, was a less difficult choice. Its greeny-gold colour and luscious, rich, almost Sauternes-like flavour really went well with the juicy Peach and Pecan Crisps.

tightly. Bake at 180°C (350°F) mark 4 for about 1 hour or until the potatoes are quite tender.

PEACH AND PECAN CRISPS

Crisp short biscuits topped with juicy peaches – delicious! Walnuts could be used to replace the pecans although they are more bitter.

50 g	pecan nuts	2 oz
50 g	plain wholemeal flour	2 oz
50 g	plain white flour	2 oz
25 g	semolina	1 oz
25 g	soft brown sugar	1 oz
75 g	polyunsaturated margarine	3 oz
	1 egg yolk	
	3 medium-sized ripe peaches *or* nectarines	
30 ml	Amaretto di Saronno (almond liqueur)	2 tbsp
15 ml	lemon juice	1 tbsp
60 ml	apricot jam	4 level tbsp
	single cream to accompany (see chicken recipe)	

Grind the pecans through a nut mouli or in a food processor. Mix with the flours, semolina and sugar. Using a fork 'cut' in the margarine until evenly blended.

Bind to a dough with the egg yolk and 15 ml (1 tbsp) water. Cover and leave to stand for 15 minutes then knead gently until just smooth.

Roll out to just under 5 mm (¼ in) thick and stamp out six rounds using a 9 cm (3½ in) fluted cutter. Place on a baking sheet. Reroll the trimmings and cut out a few crescent shapes; place on the baking sheet. Chill the pastry shapes for about 15 minutes then prick lightly with a fork. Bake at 180°C (350°F) mark 4 for about 15–20 minutes or until well browned. Cool on a wire rack.

Meanwhile wipe the peaches, cut them, unpeeled, into quarters then slice each quarter into three pieces. Place in a small bowl with the Amaretto di Saronno and lemon juice stirring well to ensure the peaches are evenly coated. Cover tightly with cling film and refrigerate for a couple of hours.

Sieve the apricot jam into a small saucepan then strain in the juices from the peaches. Warm gently until evenly blended. Then simmer until a syrupy consistency; remove from the heat. Brush each pastry round with the glaze. Arrange the peach slices on top and glaze again. Brush the pastry crescents with any remaining glaze.

Arrange the Peach and Pecan Crisps on a serving plate and decorate with the crescents. Leave in a cool place for a couple of hours before serving accompanied by single cream.

COUNTDOWN

The day before: Make and bake the pastry for the pecan crisps; cool, store in an airtight container. Prepare the broccoli mixture but don't spoon into the mould or bake yet. Leave in a bowl, cover lightly and refrigerate.

On the morning: Prepare the raspberry vinegar, strain, cool. Prepare the dressing, cover and reserve. Wash the radicchio leaves, drain, dry and refrigerate in a polythene bag. Bat out the chicken fillets, cut in half, cover and refrigerate. Cut up the spring onions, refrigerate in a polythene bag. Chop the fresh tarragon. Place in a small bowl, cover tightly and refrigerate. Grease the ring mould for the broccoli and sprinkle with crumbs; cover and leave in a cool place. Scrub the potatoes, halve and then lightly brown. Season add the garlic; cover. Store in a cool place.

About 4 pm: Prepare peaches; add the Amaretto and lemon juice.

5.30 pm: Slice the avocado into the dressing, cover and refrigerate.

Prepare the glaze and complete the Peach and Pecan Crisps.

To Serve at 8 pm

About 6.45 pm: Preheat the oven to 180°C (350°F) mark 4. Cook potatoes. Whisk the broccoli mixture and spoon into the prepared tin. Place in a *bain-marie* and put in the oven to cook.

7.30 pm: Brown the chicken pieces and complete the dish; cover and simmer for 10–15 minutes. Keep warm in a covered dish.

Just before 8 pm: Arrange the radicchio and avocado mixture on individual serving plates.

8 pm: Serve the meal.

Freezer Notes

Freeze the chicken without the cream. Thaw overnight; reheat on top of the cooker and add the cream. Freeze the broccoli mixture in a container. Thaw overnight at cool room temperature; whisk well then complete. The pecan pastries can be frozen, undecorated.

DINNER FOR A LATE SUMMER EVENING

With summer warmth in the air, this is the time for light, yet well-seasoned food. This menu combines unusual flavours in exciting ways to tempt the most exacting palate. To start, there's a delicate Warm Chicken Liver Mousseline.

To follow, we've been extravagant and used tender veal escalopes rolled up with slices of Parma ham and a piquant crunchy stuffing. A pepper ragout, well reduced to blend and soften the flavours, is the perfect accompaniment but to add colour and a balance of textures, serve a bowl of crisp stick beans as well.

To end, we felt this menu cried out for cheese and fruit, but for those with a sweet tooth, serve some luscious chocolate truffles.

Warm Chicken Liver Mousseline

The lemon and spinach sauce cuts through the richness of the chicken livers. Serve the mousseline cut into thin slices and garnished with dill.

125 g	onion	4 oz
	butter *or* polyunsaturated margarine	
225 g	chicken livers	8 oz
	1 clove garlic	
75 g	chicken breast fillet	3 oz
	2 eggs	
	1 lemon	
	salt and pepper	
142 ml	carton single cream	5 fl oz
25 g	fresh white breadcrumbs	1 oz
125 g	fresh spinach leaves	4 oz
15 ml	flour	1 level tbsp
300 ml	chicken stock	½ pint
	fresh dill to garnish (optional)	
	crusty bread to accompany	

Chop the onion then fry in 25 g (1 oz) butter until beginning to colour. Meanwhile, trim the chicken livers and divide each one into 3 or 4 pieces. Add to the pan with the crushed garlic and fry for a couple of minutes, stirring frequently. Tip into a food processor or blender and add the chicken cut into 5 or 6 pieces, the eggs, grated lemon rind and seasoning. Pour in all but 30 ml (2 tbsp) cream then blend until smooth. Turn out into a bowl then stir in the breadcrumbs. Spoon the mixture into a greased 900 ml (1½ pint) ring mould and cover tightly with foil.

Place the mousseline in a roasting tin filled with enough water to come halfway up the sides of the ring mould. Bake at 180°C (350°F) mark 4 for about 40 minutes, or until the mousseline is just firm to the touch.

Meanwhile, wash the spinach well, discarding any coarse stalks.

Place in a covered pan with the water that clings to the leaves and 25 g (1 oz) butter. Cover tightly and cook until the spinach is quite tender – about 5 minutes. Stir in the flour, stock and seasoning and bring to the boil. Cook for 1–2 minutes, then purée until smooth.

Return to the pan and add 10 ml (2 tsp) lemon juice and the remaining cream. Reheat without allowing it to boil and adjust seasoning.

Turn out the mousseline and slice thinly. Spoon a little sauce on to warm individual serving plates and top with slices of mousseline. Garnish with dill. Serve with crusty bread.

Veal Paupiettes with Basil and Parma Ham

Bat out the escalopes as thinly as possible, taking care not to split the flesh or the rice stuffing will burst out of the parcels.

75 g	brown rice	3 oz
	salt and pepper	
75 g	brazil nuts	3 oz
	1 bunch spring onions	
50 g	butter *or* polyunsaturated margarine	2 oz
30 ml	chopped fresh basil *or*	2 level tbsp
5 ml	dried basil	1 level tsp
	1 egg	
each 75–100 g	8 veal escalopes	each 3–4 oz
175 g	Parma ham	6 oz
30 ml	polyunsaturated oil	2 tbsp
15 ml	flour	1 level tbsp
225 g	onion	8 oz
150 ml	dry vermouth	¼ pint
150 ml	chicken stock	¼ pint
	fresh basil to garnish (optional)	

WINES WITH THE FOOD

Our sophisticated late summer dinner party menu has some lovely reminders of seasonal flavours and herbs that deserve summery, yet full-flavoured wines to accompany them. Sunshine may not be guaranteed with this dinner but, even if it's pouring with rain, both the food and the wine will nevertheless evoke memories of warmer evenings.

The delicious starter – rich, creamy slices of Warm Chicken Liver Mousseline – is served with a tart spinach and lemon sauce that helpfully cuts through the richness of the dish and has an almost sorrel-like acidity and intensity to it. An Italian Chardonnay did not quite suit it, but we found that an excellent fresh, green, gutsy, gooseberry-like Cépage Sauvignon from the Caves des Vignerons de Saumur in the Loire, was a perfect match, available from wine merchants and off-licence chains.

On to the Veal Paupiettes, fillets of veal filled with Parma ham, crunchy brazil nuts, fresh basil and brown rice, served with a Mixed Pepper Ragout side dish, all adding up to a softly spicy but crunchy plateful. Given the intriguing texture and flavours of the paupiettes, a warm, spicy, oak-influenced red wine seemed the best bet.

The winning wine was a spicy-truffly, yet velvet-textured '80 Barolo, from Italy, a good buy from wine merchants and supermarkets. A delicious, rich, cedary-fruity '82 Tinta da Anfora, from Portugal, also went well with the paupiettes – and both are very good value wines.

Carry on with either of these two reds for the summer cheese board, served with fresh plums, but avoid drinking wine with the Chocolate Nut Truffles, whose rich taste is best enjoyed entirely on its own.

To round off this supper try a luscious, fruity glass of Churchill Graham's Vintage Character port.

Cook the rice in plenty of boiling salted water until tender – about 30 minutes; drain. Roughly chop the brazil nuts and spring onions. Fry together in half the butter until lightly browned, then mix with the rice, basil and seasonings. Stir in the beaten egg.

Snip any fat or skin off the veal then bat out each slice between sheets of cling film until very thin. Divide each one into 2 or 3 pieces. Place a small slice of Parma ham on each piece of veal; top with stuffing and roll up to form paupiettes. Secure with wooden cocktail sticks.

Heat the oil and remaining butter in a large shallow flameproof casserole. Sprinkle the flour over the paupiettes then brown half at a time in the hot fat. Remove from the casserole and add the sliced onion and any remaining flour. Cook until golden then pour in the vermouth and stock and bring to the boil, stirring all the time to scrape any sediment off the bottom of the pan. Season lightly and replace the paupiettes.

Cover and bake at 180°C (350°F) mark 4 for about 40 minutes, or until the veal is quite tender. Bubble down the juices to thicken slightly and adjust seasoning. Keep warm, covered, in a low oven. Garnish with basil to serve.

MIXED PEPPER RAGOUT

On its own this pepper ragout tastes slightly bitter, but it really complements the veal dish.

	8 peppers, red, green and yellow mixed	
450 g	tomatoes	1 lb
30 ml	polyunsaturated oil	2 tbsp
	1 clove garlic	
	salt and pepper	

Grill the peppers, turning occasionally, until the skins are well charred. Cool slightly, then peel off the skins. Halve the peppers, discard the seeds and slice the flesh. Skin the tomatoes, quarter and seed, reserving any juices. Cut the tomato flesh into slices.

Heat the oil in a medium-sized saucepan. Add the peppers, tomatoes and juices, crushed garlic and seasoning. Cover and simmer for about 15 minutes, or until the

Late Summer line-up; left to right, Warm Chicken Liver Mousseline, Mixed Pepper Ragout with Green Stick Beans, Veal Paupiettes with Basil and Parma Ham and Chocolate Nut Truffles.

peppers are tender and the tomatoes broken down.

Uncover and bubble off any free liquid, stirring frequently as the mixture reduces; adjust seasoning. Keep warm in a covered dish in a low oven until you are ready to serve dinner.

BABY BAKED POTATOES

1.4 kg	small new potatoes	3 lb
	salt and pepper	

Simply scrub the potatoes then place in a roasting tin lined with foil. Season, then overwrap the foil to enclose the potatoes completely. Bake at 220°C (425°F) mark 7 for 45 minutes, then 180°C (350°F) mark 4 for about 30–45 minutes.

Slice the courgettes into rounds about 1 cm ($\frac{1}{2}$ in) thick. Sprinkle them lightly with salt and leave them to drain for 20 minutes. Pat dry. Sauté the crushed garlic in oil for 30 seconds only, then add the courgettes and cook them gently on one side until almost tender. Turn and cook on the other side.

Meanwhile, skin and chop the tomatoes; add to the pan with the vinegar, sugar and seasoning. Simmer until the vegetables are well done. Cool, then sprinkle with parsley to serve.

PISTACHIO PILAU

This is a highly decorative way of serving rice, perfect for a party. If pistachio nuts are not available, use chopped toasted almonds and chopped parsley to give a similar effect.

	1 small onion	
	1 clove garlic	
	polyunsaturated oil	
350 g	long-grain white rice	12 oz
	salt and pepper	
50 g	shelled pistachio nuts	2 oz

Finely chop the onion; crush the garlic. Cook in 30 ml (2 tbsp) oil until the onion is beginning to soften but not colour. Stir in the rice and 500 ml (18 fl oz) lightly salted water. Bring to the boil, stirring once, then cover and simmer until the rice is tender – about 20 minutes. Drain off any remaining water.

Meanwhile, skin the nuts and fry until golden in a little oil. Stir into the rice; season to taste. Cover and keep warm until ready to turn out and serve.

Simply exotic; clockwise from the left, Spiced Meat Skewers on a bed of Pistachio Pilau, Yogurt Sauce and Courgettes with Tomatoes.

PEACHES AND ROSE CREAM

Triple-distilled rose-water, with its heady scent and taste, goes especially well with fresh peaches. Do try a bottle for this recipe and then add it to ice creams, custards and summer fruit dishes. The bottle we bought said 'for external use only' but we were assured by the chemist that small amounts can be used in cooking. It must not be drunk neat. It is available from pharmacists.

125 g	granulated sugar	4 oz
	triple-distilled rose-water	
	6 ripe peaches	
225 g	strawberries	8 oz
150 ml	whipping cream *or* thick yogurt	5 fl oz

Dissolve the sugar in 450 ml (¾ pint) water, bring to the boil then simmer the syrup for 5 minutes. Add 5 ml (1 tsp) rose-water and the halved, peeled peaches and cook very gently, covered, for 10–15 minutes, depending on their ripeness and size. Remove the peaches, cool them a little and remove stones. Cool completely.

Meanwhile, purée the strawberries with 30–45 ml (2–3 tbsp) of the poaching syrup. Rub through a nylon sieve. Sandwich the peaches together or top each half with whipped cream or yogurt flavoured with rose-water. Place the peaches on individual plates and top with sauce.

ALMOND CIGARS

Paper-thin filo pastry can usually be found in the freezer cabinets of larger supermarkets or good delis. (Take as many whole sheets of filo pastry as you need; refreeze the rest.) If unavailable, use very thinly rolled puff pastry — you'll need about 100 g (4 oz).

100 g	ground almonds	4 oz
50 g	caster sugar	2 oz
	pinch mixed spice	
30 ml	lemon juice	2 tbsp
50 g	filo pastry (strudel leaves)	2 oz
50 g	butter	2 oz
25 g	polyunsaturated margarine	1 oz
	sifted icing sugar	

Mix together the almonds, caster sugar, mixed spice and lemon juice. Cut the sheets of filo pastry into 12.5 × 7.5 cm (5 × 3 in) oblongs. Stack them together in one pile and brush the top sheet with the butter and margarine melted together.

Roll a small spoonful of almond filling into a log shape then place along the shorter edge of the pastry and roll one sheet around this filling, making a cigar. Transfer to a greased baking sheet while buttering, filling and rolling the rest of the cigars. When all the pastries are completed brush with any remaining butter.

Bake at 180°C (350°F) mark 4 for 15–20 minutes, or until the pastries are crisp and golden. Cool and sprinkle with sifted icing sugar. Store in an airtight container.

MAKES 20–25

COUNTDOWN

The day before: Wash the salad leaves for the starter. Slice the cheese into rounds. Store both, covered, in the refrigerator. Make vinaigrette dressing. Prepare and shape mince mixture around skewers. Place on cling-film-lined baking sheets. Cover loosely and refrigerate. Make courgette and tomato dish, cover and refrigerate. Poach peaches, drain and remove stones – don't fill. Refrigerate, covered. Make Almond Cigars.
The morning: Measure rice; peel pistachio nuts. Prepare ingredients for yogurt sauce but do not mix. Make strawberry sauce.

TO SERVE AT 8 PM

About 6.30 pm: Arrange salad starters on individual plates. Cut out pitta breads and top with cheese. Mix sauce for kebabs; cut lemon. Assemble peaches.
7.30 pm: Cook rice and drain; fry nuts and keep rice hot.
7.45 pm: Grill the kebabs, place in serving dishes and keep warm. Warm the pitta bread; grill cheese toasts.
8 pm: Serve the meal.

FREEZER NOTES

The Courgettes with Tomatoes can be frozen but will be more liquid on thawing. Pack and freeze the poached, peeled peaches in their *cold* syrup. Thaw for about 6 hours then complete as directed. Freeze the Almond Cigars in a rigid container. When required thaw for 3–4 hours.

VEGETARIAN THEATRE SUPPER

This vegetarian menu has been specially designed for a night out at the theatre. These dishes need only a little last-minute finishing off to make an ideal meal after the play. (Or serve a couple of light courses before the play and save the pudding for later.)

The Mixed Vegetable Terrine is made up of tasty layers of vegetable purées baked until just set and served in slices surrounded by a fresh tomato sauce. To follow, there are vine leaves packed with rice, peanuts and leeks flavoured with a refreshing tang of lemon thyme. All the dolmas need as an accompaniment are a bright green salad and French bread baked until crisp and crusty and oozing with mustard butter.

To round off this theatre supper there's a luscious Prune and Almond Flan flavoured with brandy and studded with nuts.

MIXED VEGETABLE TERRINE

Don't be put off by the rather unappetising appearance of this terrine en bloc; when sliced, it's an appealing mix of green stripes.

350 g	parsnips	12 oz
	salt and pepper	
350 g	broccoli	12 oz
350 g	fresh Brussels sprouts	12 oz
	3 eggs	
45 ml	single cream	3 tbsp
	polyunsaturated margarine for greasing	
450 g	tomatoes	1 lb
100 g	onion	4 oz
30 ml	polyunsaturated oil	2 tbsp
5 ml	flour	1 level tsp
	1 clove garlic	
	pinch sugar	
15 ml	tomato paste	1 level tbsp
	fresh dill to garnish (optional)	

Peel the parsnips, thinly slice, then cook in boiling salted water until tender; drain well. Meanwhile, thinly slice the broccoli stalks, divide the heads into florets, wash and drain. Cook in boiling salted water until tender and drain well. Trim the sprouts, cook in boiling salted water until tender and drain.

Place each vegetable separately in the blender or food processor with one of the eggs, 15 ml (1 tbsp) cream and seasoning. Blend until smooth; adjust seasoning.

Grease and base-line an 11 × 23 cm (4½ × 9 in) non-stick loaf tin. Carefully spoon in first the broccoli mixture, then the parsnip purée and finish with a sprout layer; level the surface. Cover tightly with greased foil. Stand in a roasting tin with water to come halfway up the sides of the loaf tin. Bake at 170°C (325°F) mark 3 for about 1¼ hours, or until firm to the touch. Cool, then re-

frigerate until firm. Turn out, cover and return to the refrigerator.

Meanwhile, make the sauce. Skin, quarter and seed the tomatoes, reserving the juices. Roughly chop the tomato flesh. Finely chop the onion and cook in the oil until soft but not coloured. Stir in the flour followed by the chopped tomatoes, juices and 90 ml (6 tbsp) water. Bring to the boil, stirring. Mix in the crushed garlic, sugar, tomato paste and seasoning. Simmer for about 5 minutes. Adjust the seasoning. Cool in a bowl until ready to serve.

To serve, thinly slice the terrine and serve with the tomato sauce. Garnish with fresh dill if wished.

STUFFED VINE LEAVES

If the leaves have any holes, fold them carefully to prevent the filling bursting out.

175 g	long-grain brown rice	6 oz
	salt and pepper	
450 g	leeks	1 lb
175 g	unsalted peanuts	6 oz
125 g	no-soak dried apricots	4 oz
50 g	butter *or* polyunsaturated margarine	2 oz
30 ml	fresh chopped lemon	2 level tbsp
	or	
5 ml	dried lemon	1 level tsp
	1 lemon	
	1 egg	
227 g	packet vine leaves in brine	8 oz
450 ml	vegetable stock	¾ pint
	Greek-style natural yogurt to accompany	

Cook the rice in boiling salted water until just tender (about 30 minutes). Drain. Halve the leeks lengthwise, discarding coarse, dark leaves. Slice across into thin slices; rinse well and drain. Roughly chop the nuts; snip the apricots into small pieces. Heat the butter in a frying pan, add the leeks and nuts and fry for a few minutes until the leeks have softened. Turn out into a bowl; stir in the rice, apricots, thyme and grated lemon rind. Season well and stir in the beaten egg.

Meanwhile, drain the vine leaves and boil for 5 minutes; drain and rinse under the cold tap. Cool. Divide the stuffing between the vine leaves. Fold up to form parcels and place, seam side down, in ovenproof dishes. The parcels should be placed close together in a single layer but not jammed together too tightly. Pour over the stock with the lemon juice. Cover tightly and bake at 220°C (425°F) mark 7 for about 30 minutes until piping hot.

Serve with natural Greek-style yogurt, a green salad and the Hot Mustard Loaf.

HOT MUSTARD LOAF

If you are feeding a really hungry crowd prepare two loaves. This bread is so delicious you'll find you can eat plenty of it!

75 g	softened butter	3 oz
75 g	polyunsaturated margarine	3 oz
30 ml	wholegrain mustard	2 level tbsp
	salt and pepper	
	1 large French loaf	

Beat together the butter, margarine, mustard and seasoning. Slice the loaf into 1 cm (½ in) thick pieces and sandwich together again with the mustard butter. Wrap in foil, in one or two parcels, depending on the size of your oven. Bake at 220°C (425°F) mark 7 for about 20 minutes, or until crisp and piping hot. Serve at once.

GREEN SALAD

Have all the ingredients prepared in the refrigerator, ready to toss together at the last minute.

selection of green salad leaves
1 green pepper
½ cucumber
4 sticks celery
French dressing
wholegrain mustard

Rinse and drain the salad leaves. Finely shred the pepper, cut the cucumber into sticks and thinly slice the celery. Mix all these ingredients together and toss with a French dressing made with added mustard.

PRUNE AND ALMOND FLAN

Serve this delicious flan warm, cut into fingers.

350 g	no-soak ready-to-eat pitted prunes	12 oz
45 ml	brandy	3 tbsp
175 g	plain white flour	6 oz
50 g	ground almonds	2 oz
100 g	butter *or* polyunsaturated margarine	4 oz
60 ml	icing sugar	4 level tbsp
75 g	whole almonds	3 oz
	2 eggs	
90 ml	single cream	6 tbsp
whipped cream to accompany (optional)		

Mix the prunes with the brandy and 45 ml (3 tbsp) water, cover and leave to soak for about 6 hours.

Place the flour and ground almonds in a medium-sized bowl. Cut or rub in the fat until evenly blended, then stir in 30 ml (2 level tbsp) icing sugar. Mix to a firm dough with 30–45 ml (2–3 tbsp) cold water. Knead lightly then roll out dough and use to line a 23 cm (9 in) loose-based fluted flan tin. Bake blind until dried out and beginning to brown.

Meanwhile, blanch the whole almonds to remove the skins then toast until golden; roughly chop. Whisk together the eggs, cream, remaining icing sugar and the juices drained from the prunes. Spoon the prunes into the flan case and pour in the custard mixture; scatter over the chopped nuts. Bake at 170°C (325°F) mark 3 for about 30 minutes, or until the custard is set. Serve warm, accompanied by whipped cream if wished.

WINES WITH THE FOOD

A cool bottle of fizz makes a perfect theatre prelude, and if all you have time for is a quick glass before the show then simply seal the bottle with a champagne stopper (available from all sizeable wine merchants and department stores) and leave it in the fridge for your return. The GH tasting panel's fizz vote went to a reasonably priced delicious fresh, smoky, pineapple-like '85 Crémant de Bourgogne, that also went well with the elegant, layered, vegetarian terrine first course. Or try a more expensive but fine, fresh, herbaceous '85 Chablis with the terrine, obtainable, like the fizz, from supermarkets and good wine merchants.

On to the crunchy vine leaves, which – stuffed with brown rice, apricots, peanuts, leeks, lemon thyme and lemon – demanded a similarly spicy and full-flavoured wine, as did the accompanying Hot Mustard Loaf. Try Spain's glorious inexpensive '76 Castillo de Tiebas from the Navarra with its splendid spicy cinnamon-like palate – a perfect wine to serve.

To finish – a crunchy almond pastry flan complete with brandy-soaked prunes and an egg custard. We were happy with both an old favourite, a light, luscious flowery-grapey Moscatel de Valencia, and the richer, sweeter '83 Château La Nère, Loupiac (specialist wine merchants only).

COUNTDOWN

The day before: Prepare and bake the Vegetable Terrine, chill, turn out and return to the refrigerator overwrapped with cling film. Make the tomato sauce, cool and refrigerate covered. Make and bake the Prune and Almond Flan; when cold wrap and refrigerate.

The morning: Stuff the vine leaves and place in their cooking dish, but don't add the stock yet; cover and refrigerate. Wash the salad leaves, dry well and refrigerate in polythene bags. Cut the cucumber into sticks, slice the celery and shred the pepper, wrap separately and refrigerate. Prepare the French dressing; store in a cool place. Sandwich the loaf with mustard butter, wrap in foil and leave in a cool place until ready to bake.

TO SERVE AFTER THE THEATRE

Before you go: Take all ingredients out of the refrigerator and leave in a *cool* place. Loosely cover the flan with foil ready to reheat.

The moment you return: Turn on the oven at 220°C (425°F) mark 7. Add the stock and lemon juice to the dolmas, cover tightly and put to bake for about 30 minutes. After 10 minutes slip the wrapped bread into the oven. After 15 minutes serve the starter. After 30 minutes toss the salad ingredients and serve the main course. Reheat the flan, loosely covered, at 190°C (375°F) mark 5 for about 20 minutes.

FREEZER NOTES

Pack and freeze the tomato sauce for the terrine; thaw overnight at cool room temperature. The bread can be filled with mustard butter then wrapped and frozen. Bake (wrapped) from frozen at 220°C (425°F) mark 7 for about 30 minutes. Bake the pastry case blind, pack and freeze. Leave to thaw for 2 hours before completing the Prune and Almond Flan.

DINNER WITH A DASH OF SPICE

*T*his autumn dinner party menu is quite substantial and spicy. To start the meal we suggest an unusual combination of chicken livers and pears – the fresh tart flavour of the fruit perfectly offsets the richness of the livers. It's served cold but you could cook the livers at the last minute, complete the recipe and serve it just warm. Thin slices of pork come next, first marinated in a fragrant spice mixture, then garnished with okra and accompanied by chewy brown rice and green beans. A light refreshing blackberry sorbet rounds off the meal.

Chicken Liver Salad with Pear

Chicken livers should be lightly cooked to retain flavour and moisture. Pressing them gently while they're cooking is the best method of testing – if very soft and flabby they're raw; firm on the outside, yet soft inside, they're about right; very firm and they're over-cooked.

450 g	chicken livers	1 lb
90 ml	polyunsaturated oil	6 tbsp
15 ml	white wine vinegar	1 tbsp
5 ml	Dijon mustard	1 level tsp
	salt and pepper	
	2 small ripe pears	
15 ml	lemon juice	1 tbsp
15 ml	brandy	1 tbsp
5 ml	sugar (optional)	1 level tsp
	endive	
25 g	hazelnuts	1 oz

Trim the chicken livers and divide into large bite-sized pieces. Heat 60 ml (4 tbsp) oil in a large frying pan. Add half the livers and cook over a high heat until well-browned yet still pink inside – they should still feel slightly soft when lightly pressed with a spoon. Lift out of the pan and place in a bowl. Brown the remaining livers similarly and add to the bowl. Strain the residual oil into a jug. Whisk in the remaining oil, the vinegar, mustard and seasoning. Pour over the livers, stirring gently to mix. Cool, cover and refrigerate until required.

Peel, quarter, core and cut up the pears into small pieces. Immediately mix with the lemon juice and brandy, adding sugar if necessary. Stir well, cover tightly and refrigerate until serving time. Rinse and drain the endive and dry on kitchen paper. Tear into small pieces, then refrigerate in a polythene bag. Toast the hazelnuts under the grill; cool and roughly chop.

About 30 minutes before serving gently stir together the liver and pears (the pears will have discoloured slightly), cover and leave at room temperature. At serving time arrange the endive on individual serving plates and top with the liver mixture. Garnish with the hazelnuts.

LEMON SPICED PORK

An aromatic rather than spicy dish – the best accompaniment is simply boiled or baked brown rice. The strength of cardamoms varies greatly – the fresher the better.

900 g	pork tenderloin, fillet *or* escalopes	2 lb
	2 lemons	
	12 green cardamoms	
15 ml	ground cumin	1 level tbsp
15 ml	ground coriander	1 level tbsp
	salt and pepper	
	1 clove garlic	
90 ml	polyunsaturated oil	6 tbsp
225 g	onion	8 oz
25 g	flour	1 oz
750 ml	stock	1¼ pints
	1 large bunch watercress	
45 ml	single cream	3 tbsp

Cut the tenderloin into 1 cm ($\frac{1}{2}$ in) thick slices, divide each fillet or escalope into 2 or 3 pieces. Place between sheets of cling film, then lightly bat out all the meat. Place in a shallow glass or china dish. Grate over the lemon rinds, add the strained juice. Open the cardamom pods, remove the seeds and crush. Sprinkle these over the meat with the cumin, coriander and seasoning. Add the crushed garlic, stirring well to mix. Cover tightly and refrigerate for about 24 hours, turning occasionally.

Heat the oil in a large, shallow flameproof casserole. Life the meat out of the marinade and brown in the hot oil in 3 or 4 batches. Add the sliced onion to the pan and lightly brown. Stir in the flour and cook for 1 or 2 minutes until it begins to brown. Pour in the stock and any remaining marinade and bring to the boil. Add the finely chopped watercress and replace the meat. Cover and bake at 180°C (350°F) mark 4 for about 30 minutes or until the meat is just tender. Remove from the oven, stir in the cream and adjust seasoning.

BLACKBERRY SORBET

140 g	granulated sugar	4$\frac{1}{2}$ oz
700 g	blackberries	1$\frac{1}{2}$ lb
15 ml	Kirsch	1 tbsp
	3 egg whites	

Dissolve the sugar in 300 ml ($\frac{1}{2}$ pint) water, bring to the boil then bubble for a couple of minutes. Remove from the heat and allow to cool.

Autumn Spice; Lemon Spiced Pork with Brown Rice, served with lightly boiled Baby Okra and Green Beans.

WINES WITH THE FOOD

Before the cold and frost of midwinter set in, it is pleasant to have one last reminder of sunnier days. The Chicken Liver Salad with Pear does just that, set off by a piquant vinaigrette. A strong vinaigrette is difficult to marry wine with. Similarly, pears are not the easiest fruit to find a vinous partner for. I was convinced that the gooseberry-green Sauvignon grape would be the only one that could partner this starter but, even so, a classy Ménétou-Salon Sauvignon from the Loire couldn't cope, and neither could a cheaper Sauvignon de Touraine. What finally worked wonderfully well was a modestly priced '85 Sauvignon from the Haut Poitou cooperative. Its fresh, green, grassy-nettly character plus its lively, lemony acidity went splendidly with this dish (available from good wine merchants).

The main course of Lemon Spiced Pork was even more of a challenge. Very spicy dishes such as this, and including curry, do have vinous partners – you just have to search rather hard to find them. The GH tasting panel tried various alternatives including an ultra-powerful Zinfandel from South Africa (not California, its usual home) which, surprisingly, was too dominant for the dish. An elegant '82 Bourgogne Rouge, on the other hand, proved to be too delicate, and our choice in the end was an unusual red Côtes du Rhône, the '80 La Fiole du Chevalier d'Elbène from Séguret, whose big, spicy, herbaceous, multilayered taste was the perfect accompaniment. Alternatively try a good '82 or '83 Côtes du Rhône.

Blackberry Sorbet is a punchy and flavoursome dessert. But unless you would like to serve a small, ice-cool glass of Kirsch as an accompaniment, it is better to serve this dessert by itself, as anything this cold tends to numb the tastebuds.

Pick over the blackberries. Place in a blender or food processor with the syrup and whirl until puréed. Push the mixture through a nylon sieve; discard the pips. Stir the Kirsch into the fruit purée, then pour into a shallow freezer container. Cover and freeze until the mixture has set to a mushy consistency – about 3 hours depending on the depth of the purée. Turn out into a bowl and whisk to break down all the ice crystals. Fold in the lightly whisked egg whites, then return to the freezer container. Freeze until firm – at least 5 hours.

About $1-1\frac{1}{4}$ hours before serving transfer the sorbet to the refrigerator. Serve in individual serving dishes with Langues de Chat.

LANGUES DE CHAT

The mixture makes a lot of biscuits but they're light and delicate and if any are left over will store well for several days. Do allow the biscuits plenty of room to spread while baking or the mixture will run together forming one enormous biscuit!

75 g	polyunsaturated margarine	3 oz
75 g	caster sugar	3 oz
	1 large egg	
50 g	plain white flour	2 oz
25 g	ground almonds	1 oz

Place all the ingredients in a mixing bowl and whisk together until evenly blended. Spoon into a piping bag fitted with a 5 mm–1 cm ($\frac{1}{4}$–$\frac{1}{2}$ in) plain nozzle. Pipe out into thin 5 cm (2 in) lengths on baking sheets lined with non-stick paper; there should be about 48 biscuits. Allow them plenty of room to spread – you'll need 3 or 4 baking sheets or simply bake them in rotation, putting one batch in the oven as the last one is cooked. Bake at 200°C (400°F) mark 6 for 6–7 minutes or until tinged with colour.

Using a palette knife immediately ease the biscuits off the paper and cool on wire racks. Store them in an airtight container until required.

COUNTDOWN

Several days ahead: Make the blackberry sorbet, freeze as directed in recipe.

The day before: Prepare and bat out the pork tenderloin, add the lemon and spice mixture, cover and refrigerate. Remember to turn the meat occasionally. Make the Langues de Chat, cool and store.

The morning: Prepare and fry the chicken livers, stir in the dressing, cover. Cut up the pears, mix with the lemon and brandy, cover lightly. Rinse and dry the endive, tear into small pieces and place in a polythene bag. Refrigerate all the above ingredients. Toast the hazelnuts for the salad, cool, roughly chop, store in an airtight container. Chop the watercress for the pork recipe, refrigerate covered. Top and tail 450 g (1 lb) okra, refrigerate in a polythene bag. Top, tail and halve 700 g ($1\frac{1}{2}$ lb) French beans, refrigerate in a polythene bag.

TO SERVE AT 8 PM

About 7 pm: Preheat the oven to 180°C (350°F) mark 4. Brown the pork in several batches; complete the recipe, cover and bake.

7.15 pm: Put a large pan of salted water on to boil and cook the long-grain brown rice; drain, keep warm in a covered dish. Take all the chicken liver salad ingredients out of the refrigerator. Mix together the pear and liver mixtures.

About 7.45 pm: Boil the okra and the beans; keep warm in a low oven. Check the pork; don't add the cream yet.

Just before 8 pm: Transfer the sorbet to the refrigerator. Arrange the starter on individual plates. Stir the cream into the pork dish just before serving.

FREEZER NOTES

Do not freeze the chicken liver salad. Marinate and cook the pork, don't add the cream but cool, pack and freeze. When required thaw overnight at cool room temperature, reheat on top of the stove, then stir in the cream. Freeze the sorbet for up to six months. Pack the Langues de Chat into a rigid container and freeze. Allow to thaw for about 1 hour before serving.

Hot Pot of Hare with Sage Dumplings

You'll need a large casserole for this as the dumplings must have room to rise and become light and fluffy. Make sure that the hare is well cooked. The flesh should fall off the bone.

1.8 kg	1 large hare, jointed into 12 pieces, jointed weight	4 lb
600 ml	red wine	1 pint
	1 large orange	
60 ml	cranberry sauce	4 level tbsp
	olive oil	
350 g	onion	12 oz
	small bunch fresh sage	
	salt and pepper	
	self-raising wholemeal flour	
25 g	butter	1 oz
	about 6 sticks celery	
2.5 ml	baking powder	½ level tsp
50 g	shredded suet	2 oz

Wipe the hare joints and place them in a large bowl. Pour over the wine, adding 600 ml (1 pint) water. Finely grate half the orange rind, cover and reserve. Pare the remaining rind, cut into fine strips. Squeeze the orange and add juice and pared rind to the hare with the cranberry sauce and 45 ml (3 tbsp) oil. Slice the onion and tie half the sage together with string. Stir these into the hare mixture with plenty of seasoning. Cover tightly and leave to marinate in the refrigerator for 1–2 days, turning the meat from time to time.

Lift the hare out of the marinade and pat dry with kitchen paper. Dip the pieces in 60 ml (4 level tbsp) flour. Heat a little oil and the butter in a *large* flameproof casserole and brown the hare a few pieces at a time. Remove from the casserole and add the celery cut into 5 cm (2 in) lengths and any remaining flour. Cook for 1–2 minutes then pour in all the marinade. Bring to the boil and replace the hare. Cover tightly and bake at 170°C (325°F) mark 3 for about 2 hours, or until the hare is tender. Remove the casserole from the oven and adjust seasoning. Raise the oven temperature to 190°C (375°F) mark 5.

Mix together 125 g (4 oz) self-raising wholemeal flour, the baking powder, 15 ml (1 level tbsp) chopped sage, the reserved orange rind, the suet and seasoning. Bind to a soft dough with about 100 ml (4 fl oz) water. Knead lightly, then using floured hands roll into 12 small dumplings. Bring the casserole back to the boil. Sit the dumplings on top of the liquid and cover tightly. Bake for 30–35 minutes, or until the dumplings are well risen and fluffy.

RED CABBAGE WITH CHESTNUTS

You can use fresh chestnuts, but simmer them first in a little stock before baking them with the cabbage.

900–1.1 kg	red cabbage	2–2½ lb
175 g	onion	6 oz
125 g	streaky bacon	4 oz
	polyunsaturated oil	
300 ml	stock	10 fl oz
30 ml	wine vinegar	2 tbsp
	salt and pepper	
439 g	can whole chestnuts in water	15½ oz

Shred the cabbage finely, discarding the core. Slice the onion; cut the bacon into pieces. Heat a little oil in a medium-sized flameproof casserole; add the onion and bacon and lightly brown. Stir in the cabbage, stock, vinegar and seasoning.

Bring to the boil, cover tightly and bake at 170°C (325°F) mark 3 for 1½ hours. Gently stir in the drained chestnuts. Re-cover and return to the oven set at 190°C (375°F) mark 5 for a further 15–20 minutes. Adjust seasoning to serve.

SPROUTS AND GARLIC

Splitting the sprouts before cooking allows them to absorb the flavours of garlic and nutmeg.

900 g	Brussels sprouts	2 lb
	salt and pepper	
40 g	butter *or* polyunsaturated margarine	1½ oz
	1 clove garlic	
	grated nutmeg	

Trim and halve the sprouts. Cook in boiling salted water for about 4 minutes, or until *just* tender. Drain. Return to the pan with the fat, crushed garlic and seasoning. Stir over a moderate heat until piping hot. Grate over some nutmeg and keep warm in a covered dish.

WALNUT PEAR SLICE

Grind walnuts through a nut mouli or in a food processor until fine but not oily.

125 g	plain white flour	4 oz
	ground cinnamon	
25 g	ground walnuts	1 oz
	1 lemon	
	1 egg	
	caster sugar	
50 g	softened butter *or* polyunsaturated margarine	2 oz
45 ml	fresh brown breadcrumbs	3 level tbsp
	3 ripe pears	
	cream and yogurt mixed to accompany	

Sift the flour with 2.5 ml ($\frac{1}{2}$ level tsp) ground cinnamon on to a clean dry work surface. Sprinkle the walnuts and grated rind of $\frac{1}{2}$ lemon over the flour. Make a well in the centre and into this place the egg, 50 g (2 oz) caster sugar and the fat. With the fingertips of one hand only, pinch the ingredients from the well together until evenly blended. Draw in the flour gradually, with the help of a palette knife; knead until smooth. Wrap and chill for about 30 minutes.

Roll out the pastry to an oblong about 30.5×10 cm (12×4 in), trimming the edges. Lift the pastry on to a baking sheet; sprinkle over the breadcrumbs. Peel, quarter and core each pear; slice each quarter into 4 or 5 pieces; toss gently in a little lemon juice. Drain and arrange in overlapping lines across the dough. Sprinkle over a little sugar and cinnamon.

Bake at 190°C (375°F) mark 5 for about 30 minutes or until the pastry is well browned and crisp around the edges. Allow to cool slightly. Cut into slices; serve topped with cream and yogurt.

COUNTDOWN

Two days before: Pour the marinade over the hare joints, cover tightly and refrigerate.
The day before: Make and bake the Walnut Pear Slice. Cool, cover loosely and store in a cool place.
The morning: Cut cheese into slivers, slice the melon and prepare the dressing for the starter. Cover and refrigerate. Weigh the ingredients for the dumplings but don't mix. Prepare the cabbage, onion and bacon; cover and store in a cool place. Trim and halve the sprouts; refrigerate in a polythene bag. Peel 1.4 kg (3 lb) potatoes; cover with cold water.

TO SERVE AT 8 PM

About 5 pm: Preheat the oven to 170°C (325°F) mark 3. Brown the hare, complete and put in the oven to bake.
5.45 pm: Start the red cabbage recipe, cover and bake.
7 pm: Slice avocado then arrange the starters on individual plates. Cover *tightly*.
7.15 pm: Make dumplings, add to the hot pot and return to the oven set at 190°C (375°F) mark 5. Stir chestnuts into cabbage, re-cover and return to the oven. Boil potatoes until tender, drain, mash and keep warm, covered.
7.40 pm: Cook sprouts and complete. Keep warm, covered.
8 pm: Serve the meal. Loosely cover the Walnut Pear Slice with foil. Reheat at 180°C (350°F) mark 4 for about 20 minutes.

FREEZER NOTES

Freeze the hare after the initial 2 hours cooking time. Thaw overnight at cool room temperature. Reheat on top of the cooker, then complete as above.

HALLOWE'EN BUFFET

Menu for Twelve

TAHINI AND GARLIC DIP WITH CHEESE STICKS

SPICED LAMB BAKE

MIXED VEGETABLES

GREEN SALAD

CHOCOLATE AND RASPBERRY MERINGUE

FRUITS IN CARAMEL

Autumnal colours and spicy food are the perfect partners for a buffet party – whether you're celebrating Hallowe'en or simply getting a few friends together. To start the party, a dip for garlic lovers served with crisp cheesy sticks. It tastes equally good spooned into the piping hot jacket potatoes which accompany the Spiced Lamb Bake. Here, mildly spiced lamb is topped with an egg and nut mixture and then baked. And to end the evening what better than layers of gooey meringue speckled with chocolate and filled with raspberries and creamy yogurt? Perhaps a tangy dish of fruits in caramel?

TAHINI AND GARLIC DIP

Tahini, which is available from many delicatessens and health food stores, adds a subtle touch to the dip.

30 ml	pale tahini (sesame paste)	2 level tbsp
	juice of 1 lemon	
	1 clove garlic	
150 g	carton low-fat soft cheese	5 oz
141 g	carton natural yogurt	5 oz
284 ml	carton whipping cream	10 fl oz
	small bunch spring onions (optional)	
45–60 ml	chopped fresh parsley	3–4 level tbsp
	salt and pepper	
	sesame seeds, toasted	
	vegetable sticks to accompany	

Add 30 ml (2 tbsp) water to the tahini and mix well until evenly blended – it may take a little time for it to mix in well. Add the strained lemon juice, crushed garlic and cheese, beating well until smooth. Stir in the yogurt. Whisk the cream until it holds its shape and carefully fold into the tahini mixture.

Finely chop the spring onions, reserve a few for garnish and mix remainder with the parsley. Stir into the dip. Season to taste. Cover and chill well before serving. Garnish with the spring onions and a scattering of sesame seeds. Serve with Cheese Sticks (see recipe) and a variety of vegetable sticks.

CHEESE STICKS

These crisp cheese sticks make excellent 'dunkers' for the dip.

	1 large loaf bread (brown or white), preferably sliced	
125 g	polyunsaturated margarine	4 oz
50 g	mature Cheddar cheese	2 oz
5 ml	Dijon mustard	1 level tsp
	salt and pepper	

Remove the crusts from the bread. Roll each slice with a rolling pin to flatten completely. Mix 50 g (2 oz) of the margarine with the finely grated Cheddar cheese, mustard and seasoning. Spread evenly over the bread slices.

Cut each slice in half lengthwise and tightly roll into long cigarette shapes. Secure 4 together with cocktail sticks at each end. Trim the ends and place on baking trays. Melt the remaining margarine and brush over the bread 'sticks'. Bake at 230°C (450°F) mark 8 for 5–10 minutes or until crisp and golden brown. Serve warm or cold (remove sticks before serving).

SPICED LAMB BAKE

Just mildly spiced, this lamb bake must be served piping hot – remember the deeper the dish, the longer it takes to heat through. It's best to use two pans to prepare the lamb as there's a large quantity of meat.

175 g	whole almonds	6 oz
150 g	'no-soak' dried apricots	5 oz
	5 eating apples	
600 g	onions	$1\frac{1}{4}$ lb
75 g	polyunsaturated margarine	3 oz
1.8 kg	minced lamb	4 lb
30 ml	medium hot curry powder	2 level tbsp
45 ml	lemon juice	3 tbsp
	salt and pepper	
	6 eggs	
900 ml	milk	$1\frac{1}{2}$ pints
75 g	brown bread	3 oz
	a few flaked almonds to garnish	

Blanch and roughly chop the whole almonds; roughly chop the apricots. Peel, quarter, core and roughly chop the apple; chop the onion. Melt the margarine, add the onion and apple. Cook gently, stirring for a few minutes or until beginning to soften.

Add the lamb, increase the heat and cook quickly, stirring for a few minutes. Remove from the heat and carefully skim off any excess fat.

Stir in the curry powder, return to the heat and cook for 1–2 minutes. Add the almonds, apricots, lemon juice and seasoning. Cover and cook gently for about 20 minutes.

Meanwhile, whisk the eggs and milk together and season well. Cut the crusts from the bread, break up the slices and place in a small dish. Pour over half of the egg and milk mixture and leave to soak.

Remove the lamb from the heat, mash the bread into the milk with a fork until thoroughly broken down; stir into the lamb. Pour into two deep ovenproof dishes, level the surface with a fork. Carefully pour over the remaining milk mixture; sprinkle a few flaked almonds on the top. Bake at 180°C (350°F) mark 4 for 45–60 minutes or until the top is golden and the mince mixture piping hot. Keep warm, uncovered, in a low oven.

MIXED VEGETABLES

Gently stir the vegetables as they cook to prevent them breaking up. They should be tender yet retain a definable shape.

	1 large or 2 small cauliflowers	
450 lb	courgettes	1 lb
900 g	pumpkin	2 lb
	2 medium onions	
60 ml	polyunsaturated oil	4 tbsp
	2 cloves garlic	
20 ml	black mustard seeds	4 level tsp
10 ml	ground cardamom	2 level tsp
10 ml	paprika	2 level tsp
5 ml	ground coriander	1 level tsp
600 ml	light stock	1 pint
30 ml	creamed coconut	2 level tbsp
	salt and pepper	

Divide the cauliflower into florets, thickly slice the courgettes, cut the pumpkin into chunks, discarding the rind and seeds; slice the onion.

Heat the oil in a large flameproof casserole, add the onion and crushed garlic and cook until beginning to soften and colour. Stir in the cauliflower and courgettes. Cook for a few minutes, stirring occasionally, then add the mustard seeds, cardamom, paprika and coriander. Stir thoroughly to blend the spices and cook for 1–2 minutes. Reduce the heat, add the pumpkin and stock stirring to mix. Cover and simmer until the vegetables are tender, about 15–20 minutes, taking care not to break up the pumpkin. Mix the creamed coconut with 15 ml (1 tbsp) hot water to form a smooth paste. Add to the vegetables and adjust seasoning. Cook for a further 2–3 minutes.

WINES WITH THE FOOD

Midwinter entertaining on a large scale need not be an expensive experience, as this informal Hallowe'en buffet demonstrates. Our starter, the soft, creamy Tahini and Garlic Dip, does not in any case make the perfect accompaniment to a pricy white wine. Instead, what is needed is an easy-going, inexpensive white that, besides coping with the strongly flavoured Tahini, also makes a good aperitif.

Having toyed with various dry French white wines, the GH tasting team plumped for the light, fresh, fruity Bulgarian Chardonnay that is a widely available bargain buy and yet still has the guts to cope with the tahini. Do not, however, expect too much Chardonnay flavour from this wine – the Bulgarians still have a long way to go before they challenge the Burgundians.

The Spiced Lamb Bake with its crunchy almonds and soft, spicy-fruity flavours deserved a warming winter red to accompany it. But as the GH team surprisingly discovered, rioja and other robust reds overpowered the gently spicy character of the dish. Instead, an '83 Buzet, from a region southeast of Bordeaux, with a lively black- and redcurrant-like taste and sufficient backbone to cope with the exotic spices was the perfect partner. Obtainable from supermarkets and wine merchants.

To finish, the glorious crunchy Chocolate and Raspberry Meringue plus the sweet Fruits in Caramel needed a sweet yet fruity pudding wine. The answer was with a luscious, peachy '84 Clos St Georges, a very reasonably priced Graves Supérieures.

Substantial Hallowe'en Supper: two Spiced Lamb Bakes, a huge dish of Mixed Vegetables and a refreshing Green Salad.

CHOCOLATE AND RASPBERRY MERINGUE

Make twice the recipe to feed 12. Sandwich together at least an hour before serving to give the meringue time to soften.

50 g	plain chocolate	2 oz
	4 egg whites	
225 g	caster sugar	8 oz
142 ml	carton double cream	5 fl oz
141 g	carton natural yogurt	5 oz
350 g	frozen raspberries, thawed	12 oz
	icing sugar	

Finely grate the chocolate and set aside. Whisk the egg whites until stiff but not dry. Add 20 ml (4 level tsp) of the sugar and whisk again until the mixture regains its former stiffness and is shiny. Carefully fold in the remaining sugar with the chocolate. Spoon or pipe into two 23 cm (9 in) circles on trays lined with non-stick paper.

Bake at 180°C (350°F) mark 4 for about 30 minutes, exchanging baking tray positions if necessary. Lower heat to 100°C (200°F) gas mark low and bake for a further 1 hour until firm and dry. Peel away the paper, place on cooling racks and leave until cold.

Whisk the cream until it holds its shape, add the yogurt; whisk again. Carefully fold in 125 g (4 oz) of the raspberries. Use to sandwich the meringue rounds together. Refrigerate for at least 1 hour before serving with raspberry sauce.

To prepare the sauce, push the remaining raspberries through a nylon sieve. Add 60 ml (4 level tbsp) sifted icing sugar, 15 ml (1 level tbsp) at a time, beating thoroughly. Chill and serve.

Fruits in Caramel

225 g	granulated sugar	½ lb
450 g	kumquats	1 lb
	10 tangerines	
	8 ripe pears	
60 ml	brandy *or* rum	4 tbsp
	single cream to accompany (optional)	

Make the caramel by placing 150 ml (¼ pint) cold water in a deep heavy-based pan with the sugar. Heat gently, stirring occasionally until the sugar dissolves, then increase the heat and boil the syrup until it turns a dark golden caramel colour – don't let it blacken or it will be very bitter.

Have ready 150 ml (¼ pint) hot water. Draw the pan aside and quickly add all of the hot water (be careful as it will spit). Bring slowly to the boil, stirring to dissolve any solidified caramel, and then boil for 2–3 minutes until it has a syrupy consistency. Add the rinsed and trimmed kumquats and heat gently for 2–3 minutes. Pour into a heat-proof bowl and allow to cool.

Peel and quarter the pears, remove the cores and slice thickly. Add to the cooled syrup. Remove the peel and pith from the tangerines, working over the bowl of cooled caramel to catch the juices. Segment the tangerines and add to the cooled syrup. Add the brandy, cover and chill before serving.

Countdown

Two days before: Make the meringues. Cool and store in airtight containers.

The day before: Make the Tahini and Garlic Dip, omitting the spring onion, parsley and sesame seed garnish. Prepare the cheese sticks, but don't brush with margarine or bake yet. Cover and refrigerate.

On the morning: Make the caramel sauce, add kumquats, allow to cool. Blanch and roughly chop the almonds, roughly chop the apricots, cover and set aside. Prepare the Spiced Lamb Bake as far as but not including the addition of the egg and milk. Cool and refrigerate. Prepare the cauliflower, courgettes and pumpkin, pack in polythene bags and refrigerate. Wash, drain and dry salad ingredients of your choice, refrigerate in polythene bags. Prepare a vinaigrette dressing. Scrub potatoes for baking. Pick over the raspberries, cover and refrigerate. Make the raspberry sauce, cover and chill. Add the tangerines, pears and brandy or rum to the sauce, cover and chill.

To Serve at 8 pm

About 6 pm: Bake cheese sticks. Thread potatoes on to skewers and bake. Add spring onions, parsley and sesame seeds to dip. Cover and chill. Soak the bread in the egg and milk. Reheat the Spiced Lamb Bake, complete and bake.

6.30 pm: Fill the meringue, refrigerate until needed.

6.45 pm: Place lamb mixture into dishes. Smooth the top and pour over egg and milk. Sprinkle a few flaked almonds on top and bake.

7.30 pm: Cook the vegetables.

7.45 pm: Reheat cheese sticks in the oven, uncovered. Toss salad in the vinaigrette dressing.

8 pm: Serve the meal.

Freezer Notes

Pack and freeze the unfilled meringue rounds. Pack and freeze cheese sticks before brushing with margarine or baking. Bake from frozen. Freeze the lamb mixture without the topping. To use, thaw overnight.

ROAST PARSNIPS

Blanching parsnips before roasting keeps them moist and succulent.

900 g	parsnips	2 lb
	salt	
	polyunsaturated oil	

Peel the parsnips and cut into *fat* finger-shaped pieces. Cover with cold salted water and bring to the boil; bubble for 1 minute, drain. Immediately heat a thin covering of oil in a roasting tin. Add the parsnips then roast at the top of the oven at 200°C (400°F) mark 6 for $1\frac{1}{4}$–$1\frac{1}{2}$ hours or until golden and crisp. Turn and baste two or three times while cooking. Keep warm, uncovered, in a low oven.

CREAMED BUTTON ONIONS

700 g	small button onions	$1\frac{1}{2}$ lb
	salt and pepper	
40 g	polyunsaturated margarine	$1\frac{1}{2}$ oz
25 g	flour	1 oz
150 ml	milk	$\frac{1}{4}$ pint
5 ml	English made mustard	1 level tsp
30 ml	chopped fresh parsley	2 level tbsp

Soak the onions in warm water for about 15 minutes – this helps to loosen the skins. Skin, trimming the root ends carefully; do not cut the root right off or the onion will fall apart.

Cook in boiling salted water in a covered pan for 15–20 minutes or

Keep up tradition with, clockwise from the left, Roast Rib of Beef, Yorkshire Puddings, Green Cabbage, Creamed Button Onions, Roast Parsnips and Roast Potatoes.

Lunch on Sunday is a wonderful excuse to bring out those full-bodied bottles of red wine that you may well have been waiting to drink all summer. Working on my theory that whatever is spent per head on food should also be spent on wine (well roughly anyway!) it was obvious that the magnificent rib of roast beef deserved a special red to accompany it. If roast beef is the most traditional British dish then claret, the red wine of Bordeaux, is this country's most traditional wine. Before every English *vigneron* exclaims in horror I should just mention that the GH tasting team did try several English wines, both as an aperitif and with the roast beef, and none was felt to be exactly right, either for the occasion or the meat.

Of the three clarets that we tried with the roast beef plus its traditional and flavoursome trimmings of roast potatoes, roast parsnips and creamed button onions (the last two vegetables surprisingly sweet served like this), the favourite was the excellent Château Tourteau-Chollet '83 from the Graves, available from supermarkets and good wine merchants. This claret with its rich, firm, grassy flavour packed with lots of blackcurranty fruit and even a touch of cedarwood on the finish is a very good buy. It also has enough backbone to cope with the sweetness of the vegetables. Alternatively, if you can afford it, try the delicious velvety, ripe and full '81 Ramage La Batisse, a wonderful claret, and an up-and-coming *cru bourgeois* from the Haut-Médoc. (Fine wine merchants only.)

The English pudding to finish off this traditional meal was a delicious crisp Apple Charlotte served with nutmeg custard. Half bottles of Robert Mondavi's widely available fresh, sherbetty, aniseedy Moscato d'Oro were an excellent accompaniment.

until just tender. Drain off the liquor reserving 200 ml (7 fl oz). Place the onions in a serving dish. Cover and keep warm.

Melt the margarine in a small saucepan. Stir in the flour and cook for a few seconds. Remove from the heat and stir in the milk followed by the reserved juices. Bring to the boil stirring all the time. Bubble for 1–2 minutes then stir in the mustard and parsley and season to taste. Stir the sauce gently through the onions. Cover and keep warm until required.

GREEN CABBAGE

900 g–1.1 kg	green cabbage	2–2½ lb
	salt and pepper	
	butter *or* polyunsaturated margarine (optional)	

Cut up the cabbage into bite-sized pieces, discarding the core; alternatively divide into wedges. Rinse and drain. Cook in boiling salted water for 1–2 minutes only. Drain, season with plenty of milled pepper and add a little fat if wished. Keep warm, covered, in a low oven.

QUICK APPLE CHARLOTTE

700 g	eating apples	1½ lb
700 g	cooking apples	1½ lb
75 g	butter *or* polyunsaturated margarine	3 oz
2.5 ml	ground cinnamon	½ level tsp
	1 lemon	
45 ml	apricot jam	3 level tbsp
60 ml	caster sugar	4 level tbsp
400 g	loaf mixed-grain bread (unsliced) or a small brown loaf	14 oz

Peel, quarter, core and thickly slice the eating and cooking apples. Place in a large saucepan

with 25 g (1 oz) margarine and the cinnamon. Add the grated lemon rind and the strained juice with the jam and half the sugar. Cover the pan tightly and cook gently until the apples are beginning to soften – about 15 minutes. Uncover and stir over a high heat for a minute or two to drive off excess moisture. (The apples should not be completely broken down.)

Meanwhile make 50 g (2 oz) breadcrumbs from the loaf and stir into the apple mixture. Turn into a 1.7 litre (3 pint) shallow ovenproof dish. Cut about nine slices of bread 2.5–5 mm ($\frac{1}{8}$–$\frac{1}{4}$ in) thick and remove the crusts. Spread one side of each slice with the remaining margarine and sprinkle the remaining sugar over this side. Halve each slice diagonally then arrange sugar-side up over the apple until it is more or less completely covered. Don't overlap the slices too closely or they will not crisp up properly.

Place the dish on a baking sheet and bake at 220°C (425°F) mark 7 for about 20 minutes – the bread should be brown and crisp. Cool for about 10 minutes. Serve with home-made custard.

COUNTDOWN

The day before: Peel the onions, dry with kitchen paper, refrigerate in a polythene bag. Prepare the apple purée, stir in the crumbs, cool, cover and refrigerate. Make the custard, adding nutmeg to taste, and refrigerate.

Early on Sunday morning: Place the apple mixture in the baking dish, top with bread but don't bake yet. Peel the potatoes and parsnips, cover with cold water, leave in a cool place. Cut up the cabbage, rinse and drain, refrigerate in a polythene bag. Prepare the Yorkshire pudding batter, cover and leave to stand. Calculate the cooking time for the beef – 15 minutes per 450 g (1 lb) for medium rare, a little less for rare and a little longer for a well-done roast.

To Serve at 1.30 pm

10.45 am: Preheat the oven to 200°C (400°F) mark 6.
11–11.30 am: Put the beef and potatoes in to roast. Blanch the parsnips and put in the oven to roast. Remember to baste and turn all these ingredients at regular intervals.
12.30 pm: Boil the onions, prepare the sauce and mix together. Cover and keep warm in a low oven.

12.45 pm: Put the water on for the cabbage; boil, drain, cover and keep warm. Check the meat, roast potatoes and parsnips; keep warm uncovered.
1 pm: Raise the oven temperature to 220°C (425°F) mark 7 and put in the Yorkshire pudding tins. Meanwhile give the batter another whirl, pour into the tins and bake. It is only possible to raise the oven temperature if you have a double oven or somewhere to keep the meat and other dishes warm. If not, bake the Yorkshire puddings while roasting the meat and vegetables – the time plan can then be started 30 minutes later. Make the gravy.
1.30 pm: Serve the meal.
Put in the Charlotte to bake; test after 20 minutes and leave to stand for at least 10 minutes before serving. Reheat the custard without boiling or serve it chilled.

Freezer Notes

It's best to prepare all the recipes freshly for the roast meal – the joint of beef can be frozen if wished. Pack and freeze the apple purée for the Charlotte. Thaw before completing the recipe as directed.

INFORMAL FRENCH SUPPER

Menu for Four

MUSSELS IN TOMATO SAUCE

CHEESE AND LEEK TART

LEAFY GREEN SALAD

APPLE AND CALVADOS SORBET

CARAMEL TUILES

French meals seem to fall into two categories – relaxed and homely or elegant and formal. We've chosen the former for this French dinner party menu with delicious recipe ideas from northern France.

With the sea nearby, mussels are found in abundance and make a truly wonderful starter. Next on the menu is a rich leek tart with a creamy Camembert custard filling. In true French fashion, it's served alone followed by a crisp salad then a variety of cheeses. Try some regional cheeses such as Maroilles, a creamy, semi-hard cheese with a strong flavour and pungent aroma, or perhaps a young goat's cheese – the flavour intensifies with age.

A delicate Apple and Calvados Sorbet completes the meal – but be warned, the Calvados, distilled in Normandy, gives it quite a kick. Serve accompanied by Caramel Tuiles.

MUSSELS IN TOMATO SAUCE

Mussels should always be bought alive; check by tapping any open shells with the handle of a knife and discard any that don't close immediately. They are sold either by the 450 g (1 lb) or 600 ml (1 pint). Below we allow about 12–14 good-sized mussels per person.

1.1 kg/ 2.8 litres	fresh mussels	2½ lb/ 5 pints
	salt and pepper	
40 g	coarse oatmeal	1½ oz
450 g	ripe tomatoes	1 lb
125 g	shallots	4 oz
15 ml	polyunsaturated oil	1 tbsp
	1 clove garlic	
5 ml	dried thyme	1 level tsp
15 ml	tomato paste	1 level tbsp
5 ml	white wine vinegar	1 tsp
300 ml	dry cider	½ pint
15 ml	chopped fresh parsley	1 level tbsp
	French bread to accompany	

Pick over the mussels, discarding any that have open or damaged shells. Scrub the shells under cold running water to remove any sand or grit. Then, using a small knife, trim away the beard (the weed caught between the closed shells) and scrape off any barnacles.

Place the prepared mussels in a large bowl, cover with *cold* salted water and sprinkle over the oatmeal. Leave in a cool place overnight, then wash and drain well. Check all the mussels are still tightly closed.

Skin, seed and roughly chop the tomatoes (reserving any juices). Skin and thinly slice the shallots. Heat the oil in a large saucepan and add the shallots, crushed garlic and thyme. Cook, stirring, for 1–2 minutes, then stir in the tomatoes and any juices, the tomato paste, vinegar, seasoning and cider. Add the mussels, bring to the boil, cover tightly and cook over a moderate heat for 5–7 minutes, shaking the pan occasionally, until all the shells are open.

Using a slotted spoon, transfer the mussels to a warmed serving dish, discarding any unopened shells. Cover with foil to keep the mussels warm while you complete the dish.

Bring the cooking liquor back to the boil and boil rapidly for 1–2 minutes. Adjust the seasoning then pour over the mussels. Garnish with the chopped parsley and serve with lots of warm French bread.

CHEESE AND LEEK TART

Butter gives a wonderful flavour to the pastry. Polyunsaturated margarine can be used but cut it in with a fork rather than rubbing in by hand.

175 g	plain white flour	6 oz
	salt and pepper	
100 g	butter	4 oz
5 ml	Parmesan cheese	1 level tsp
	2 eggs and 1 egg yolk	
450 g	trimmed leeks	1 lb
15 ml	polyunsaturated oil	1 tbsp
	pinch nutmeg	
75 g	Camembert	3 oz
142 ml	carton single cream	5 fl oz
50 ml	milk	2 fl oz

Place the flour and salt in a bowl. Rub in 75 g (3 oz) butter until the mixture resembles fine bread-crumbs. Stir in the Parmesan cheese. Bind the ingredients together with the egg yolk and about 30 ml (2 tbsp) water. Knead lightly then wrap and chill the pastry for about 15 minutes.

Meanwhile, trim the leeks, cut into thin rings and wash well. Heat

the remaining butter and oil in a large sauté pan, add the leeks and nutmeg. Cover and cook gently for about 10 minutes, or until the leeks have softened but not coloured; cool. Meanwhile, roll out the pastry on a lightly floured surface and use to line a 20.5 cm (8 in) flan ring, placed on a baking sheet; chill for about 15 minutes. Bake blind at 200°C (400°F) mark 6 for about 12 minutes or until set but not browned.

Remove the rind from the Camembert, then roughly chop or mash with a fork. Place in a bowl with the cream and whisk until almost smooth. Whisk in the eggs and milk and season well. Using a slotted spoon, pile the leeks into the baked flan case then pour over the custard mixture. Bake at 180°C (350°F) mark 4 for about 35 minutes or until just set. Stand for about 10 minutes before serving.

Leafy Green Salad

	$\frac{1}{4}$ head Chinese leaves	
	$\frac{1}{4}$ cos lettuce	
	2 heads chicory	
15 ml	white wine vinegar	1 tbsp
15 ml	Dijon mustard	1 level tbsp
	salt and pepper	
45 ml	olive oil	3 tbsp
30 ml	polyunsaturated oil	2 tbsp

Wash, dry and roughly shred the Chinese leaves and lettuce; wash and trim the chicory, separate into leaves. Refrigerate all these ingredients in polythene bags until required.

Meanwhile, whisk together the vinegar, mustard and seasoning. Add the oils and whisk until well

Mussels in Tomato Sauce

Wines with the Food

Our mussels were cooked in cider, plus tomatoes, shallots and garlic, so, naturally, the GH tasting panel tried a range of ciders with this delicious, tangy seafood dish. Surprisingly, none could cope with the combined flavours of the sea, garlic and shallots so we moved on to wine. Once again, the mussels overpowered even Muscadet, the traditional Loire accompaniment to *moules marinières*, and a crisp Bordeaux sec. Eventually, we voted unanimously for a wonderful refreshing, grassy-nettly '85 Sauvignon du Haut Poitou from the cooperative.

On to the Cheese and Leek Tart which needed a firm but fruity red to stand up to its rich flavour. We tried several with this dish but the best by far was the delicious, deep purple, soft, velvety, seductive, spicy '85 Château du Grand Moulas, one of the finest Côtes du Rhône there is. This reasonably priced wine is available from good wine merchants.

The gloriously strong selection of French cheeses to follow needed a red with more age and staying power, and a ridiculously cheap Portuguese '82 Bairrada with its warm, spicy taste proved ideal.

Apple and Calvados Sorbet is not the easiest pudding for those whose palates, including my own, like a glass of wine with every course. But its earthy, sweet apple and calvados taste went well with the '80 Château Septy Monbazillac, obtainable from supermarkets and good wine merchants, whose earthy *crème brûlée*-like flavour echoed that of the sorbet. We did have the odd dissenting GH palate, however, that preferred the peachy, honeyed, aniseed-like '84 Domaine de Coyeaux, an upmarket widely available and pricier Muscat de Beaumes de Venise.

MAXIMUM IMPACT, MINIMUM FUSS

Menu for Eight

ARTICHOKE MOUSSE

LOINS OF LAMB WITH OATMEAL

BAKED POTATO PUREE

ROAST ONIONS

STEAMED SPROUTS

SLICED CARROTS

THREE FRUIT SALAD

The perfect dinner party menu must be one that provides a different and impressive meal with minimum last-minute effort. This menu fits the bill nicely; the main preparations are done the day before, leaving just the finishing touches for the few moments before the guests sit down. An unusual Jerusalem Artichoke Mousse, its delicate flavour complemented by crisp bacon and watercress, is followed by slices of boned stuffed lamb. And to finish there's a tangy and colourful Three Fruit Salad.

ARTICHOKE MOUSSE

Jerusalem artichokes have a wonderful, almost earthy, flavour. Buy fairly even-sized ones; the knobbly types are beasts to peel and can be wasteful.

700 g	Jerusalem artichokes	1½ lb
	lemon juice	
450 ml	light stock	¾ pint
	salt and pepper	
15 ml	powdered gelatine	1 level tbsp
142 ml	carton double *or* whipping cream	¼ pint
	2 egg whites	
125 g	streaky bacon	4 oz
	1 bunch watercress	
	French bread to accompany	

Peel the artichokes, covering immediately with water and a dash of lemon juice. Drain and thinly slice. Place in a medium-sized saucepan with the stock, 30 ml (2 tbsp) lemon juice and the seasoning. Bring to the boil, cover and simmer until very tender – about 40 minutes (there should be little liquid). Cool slightly. Purée in a food processor or electric blender until smooth. Pour out into a large bowl; leave to cool.

Meanwhile, place 45 ml (3 tbsp) water in a small bowl. Sprinkle over the gelatine. Leave to soak for at least 10 minutes or until sponge-like in texture. Dissolve by standing the basin in a pan of simmering water,

131

Stir the liquid gelatine into the cold artichoke purée. Lightly whip the cream and stir into the artichokes with the egg whites, whisked until stiff but not dry. The mixture has a slightly separated appearance. Spoon into an oiled 1.1 litre (2 pint) stainless ring mould. Cover and refrigerate to set – about 3 hours.

Meanwhile, grill the bacon until crisp and golden. Snip into small pieces discarding the rind. Store in a cool place. Rinse and drain the watercress, divide into small sprigs removing any coarse stalks. Refrigerate in a polythene bag. Turn out the mousse for serving and garnish with the watercress and bacon.

LOINS OF LAMB WITH OATMEAL

The joints are trimmed of all excess fat and then the oatmeal mops up the rest. It's easy to bone the lamb yourself but, given prior warning, most butchers will do it for you.

two 1.1 kg	loins of lamb	two 2½ lb
150 g	packet low-fat soft cheese	5 oz
30 ml	chopped fresh thyme	2 level tbsp
	or	
5 ml	dried thyme	1 level tsp
	2 cloves garlic, crushed	
	salt and pepper	
	flour	
	1 egg, beaten	
125 g	medium oatmeal	4 oz
	polyunsaturated oil	
600 ml	stock	1 pint
	sherry	
	fresh thyme to garnish (optional)	

Well planned preparation is the key to this impression of effortless ease. Clockwise from the top: Baked Potato Purée, Steamed Sprouts, Sliced Carrots, Loin of Lamb with Oatmeal and Roast Onions.

WARMING WINTER SUPPER

A warming dinner for a cold winter evening, this menu for four will provide a meal that you and your guests will want to linger over for hours. A lot of the preparation can be done on the day before, so this menu would be ideal for a mid-week dinner party. The duckling, flavoured with apples and cranberry sauce, is served with a selection of simply cooked vegetables. Brown Bread Lemon Ice Cream, a special treat for all ice cream fans, makes a pleasing end to the meal.

SCALLOP AND BROCCOLI SALAD

Poach the scallops for the minimum of time to ensure they remain succulent and juicy. The flavour of sesame oils can be quite strong so add with care.

275–350 g	4 large scallops, total weight	10–12 oz
100 ml	white wine	4 fl oz
	slices onion	
	bay leaf	
	salt and pepper	
	sesame oil	
225 g	broccoli	½ lb
	sesame seeds, toasted	
	brown bread and butter	

R inse and drain the scallops. Place in a small saucepan with the wine, onion, bay leaf and seasoning. Bring slowly to the boil, cover and simmer gently for about 2 minutes only or until the scallops are just firm to the touch. Remove from the heat and leave in the cooking juices to cool slightly – about 10 minutes. Lift the scallops out of the juices using a draining spoon. Thinly slice the flesh discarding any membrane or black particles. When quite cold cover tightly with cling film and refrigerate.

Bubble down the cooking juices until about 60 ml (4 tbsp) remains. Strain into a bowl and whisk in sesame oil to taste – about 5 ml (1 tsp) – too much oil will overpower the flavour of the scallops. Adjust seasoning, cool, cover and refrigerate.

Meanwhile, trim off any coarse

stalks from the broccoli; divide the heads into small florets. Wash well and drain. Steam the florets until just tender – about 10 minutes – then immediately rinse under the cold tap to 'set' the bright colour. Drain, then refrigerate covered.

About 30 minutes before serving arrange scallops and broccoli on individual serving plates. Spoon over the dressing and sprinkle with sesame seeds.

Serve with rolls of brown bread and butter filled with some sesame seeds and then toasted.

BRAISED DUCKLING WITH APPLE

It's best to prepare this dish the day ahead so that the fat can be skimmed off the juices the next day. Just crisp up the duckling skin before serving.

each 400 g	4 duckling portions – preferably breast portions	each 14 oz
450 g	cooking apples	1 lb
450 g	onions	1 lb
60 ml	polyunsaturated oil	4 tbsp
400 ml	stock	$\frac{3}{4}$ pint
150 ml	apple juice	$\frac{1}{4}$ pint
60 ml	cranberry sauce	4 level tbsp
	salt and pepper	
20 ml	arrowroot	4 level tsp
	fried apple slices	
	watercress sprigs	

Trim the duckling of any excess fat and halve each joint. Place on a grill rack and grill under a moderate heat for about 15 minutes or until well browned and a lot of fat has been drawn off. Pat the duckling pieces with kitchen paper to remove all fat traces.

Meanwhile peel, quarter, core and slice the apples; slice the onion. Heat the oil in a large flameproof casserole; add the apple and onion and fry for 2–3 minutes. Stir in the stock, apple juice, cranberry sauce and seasoning. Bring to the boil then add the duckling. Cover and bake at 180°C (350°F) mark 4 for about 50 minutes or until the duckling is tender. Using draining spoons, lift out the duckling. Strain the cooking juices into a heatproof jug, reserve the apple and onion slices and place in a covered dish with the duckling. Refrigerate the juices and duckling overnight.

The next day remove all fat from the juices. Reheat the juices in a flameproof casserole. Replace the duckling and apples etc. Cover

tightly and reheat at 200°C (400°F) mark 6 for about 30 minutes.

Using draining spoons place the duckling on a grill rack. Grill under a high heat to brown the skin. Keep warm, loosely covered, in a low oven. Meanwhile mix the arrowroot to a smooth paste with a little water. Add to the pan juices and bring to the boil stirring; bubble for 1 minute. Adjust seasoning and spoon a little over the duckling for serving. Pour the remainder into a sauce-boat to serve separately. Garnish the duckling with apple slices and watercress sprigs.

PUREE POTATOES

The best accompaniment to serve with the rich duckling juices.

900 g	old potatoes	2 lb
25 g	butter *or* polyunsaturated margarine	1 oz
75 ml	milk	3 fl oz
	salt and pepper	

Peel the potatoes, cut into large chunks then boil until tender. Drain well. Mash well then beat in the fat, warm milk and seasoning to taste. Keep warm in a covered dish.

STEAMED GREEN BEANS

Choose either bobby or French beans, both readily available. Bobby beans rarely require stringing and although plumper in appearance than French beans, cook in about the same time.

450 g	green beans	1 lb
	salt and pepper	
	butter *or* polyunsaturated margarine	

Top, tail and halve the beans, stringing first, if necessary. Place in a colander over a pan of boiling salted water – cover tightly and steam until tender. Add a little butter, season and keep warm, covered.

GLAZED CARROTS

As the liquid evaporates keep an eye on the carrots as they tend to stick to the bottom of the pan.

700 g	carrots	1½ lb
25 g	butter *or* polyunsaturated margarine	1 oz
2.5 ml	sugar	½ level tsp
	salt and pepper	
	snipped parsley to garnish	

Pare the carrots and cut into small barrel shapes. Place in a medium sized saucepan and just cover with cold water. Add the fat, sugar and seasoning. Bring to the boil and simmer, uncovered, until the carrots are just tender and all the liquid has evaporated – about 25 minutes. Shake the pan occasionally to prevent the carrots sticking to the pan – they should be shiny and tinged with brown. Keep warm in a covered dish. Garnish with parsley for serving.

BROWN BREAD LEMON ICE CREAM

30 ml	custard powder	2 level tbsp
100 g	soft light brown sugar	4 oz
300 ml	milk	½ pint
	1 lemon	
142 ml	carton double cream	¼ pint
142 ml	carton single cream	¼ pint
	1 egg white	
30 ml	polyunsaturated oil	2 tbsp
25 g	butter	1 oz
125 g	fresh brown breadcrumbs	4 oz

Mix the custard powder and half the sugar to a smooth paste with a little milk. Bring the remaining milk almost to the boil. Stir into the custard powder then return to the pan. Bring to the boil stirring all the time, cook for 2 minutes; pour out into a bowl and cool slightly. Whisk in the finely grated lemon rind with 45 ml (3 tbsp) strained lemon juice. Complete cooling. Whisk the creams together until they just begin to hold their shape. Whisk the custard until smooth then gently whisk in the creams. Fold in the stiffly whisked egg white. Spoon into a freezer container and freeze until mushy – about 2 hours.

Meanwhile heat the oil and butter in a frying pan; add the crumbs and remaining sugar and cook over a moderate heat, stirring occasionally, until the crumbs brown well and begin to crisp. This can take 15 minutes. Turn into a bowl; cool.

When the ice cream is mushy give it a good whisk to break down most of the ice crystals. Stir in the cold crumbs. Return to the freezer and freeze until firm – about 4 hours. Allow the ice cream to soften in the refrigerator for about 1½–2 hours before serving.

Wines with the Food

Midwinter dining calls for wines blessed with lively, positive flavours.

The starter of sweet scallop meat and crunchy broccoli is served with a light, toasty sesame oil dressing and any classic French aperitif or first-course wine would probably suffer from this unusual combination of flavours. So we opted for a big, bouncy California wine instead; Robert Mondavi's 1982 Fumé Blanc, made from the gooseberry-green Sauvignon grape, whose higher alcohol level and pungent, fresh, green, oaky smell and taste would be just the ticket.

Braised Duckling served with a sweetish apple and onion sauce with the merest touch of cranberry, needs a big, rich, fruity winter red to match its flavours. I have been most impressed with the 1981 Châteauneuf-du-Pape, Les Couversets, from J R Quiot, available from supermarkets, and although it has increased slightly in price, I still think it is delicious and a good buy. 1981 was a good year in the southern Rhône, which explains why we all enjoyed Les Couversets' full purple colour plus that ripe, gutsy, peppery fruit that is the hallmark of a good Rhône wine.

The tangy Brown Bread Lemon Ice Cream needed a luscious dessert wine with a similar balance between fruit and acidity to partner it. A ripe German wine from an excellent year was the answer and we plumped for a sweet, pineappley '76 Hattenheimer Schützenhaus Riesling Auslese from Karl J Molitor, expensive but worth it from specialist wine merchants. Alternatively, if you are trying to keep costs down, you could try the delicious, rich pudding wine – 1983 Clos St Georges, Graves Supérieures. This wonderful, sweet, peachy, golden wine would go well with the ice cream and is so modestly priced, you can order two.

Countdown

The day before: Prepare and cook the duckling; strain off the cooking juices and refrigerate as directed. Make the brown bread ice cream, freeze.

On the morning: Prepare and cook the scallops, broccoli and dressing; refrigerate separately. Prepare bread and butter rolls filled with toasted sesame seeds, refrigerate covered. Peel potatoes; cover with cold water and store in a cool place. Prepare beans, refrigerate in a polythene bag. Prepare the carrots, refrigerate in a polythene bag; snip parsley, refrigerate covered. Wash watercress sprigs, dry, refrigerate in a polythene bag.

To Serve at 8 pm

6.45 pm: Preheat oven to 200°C (400°F) mark 6. Skim duckling juices then reheat in a flameproof casserole. Replace duckling and apples, cover and place in the oven to reheat.

About 7.15 pm: Boil potatoes; put carrots on to cook.

7.30 pm: Place ice cream in refrigerator to soften. Arrange scallops, broccoli and dressing on serving plates. Mash potatoes, cover and keep warm. Check carrots, cover and keep warm. Steam beans, add a little butter, cover and keep warm. Grill duckling and thicken juices. Toast brown bread rolls.

8 pm: Serve the meal.

Freezer Notes

Do not freeze the Scallop and Broccoli Salad. Cook the duckling, strain off the juices and refrigerate overnight. Skim as directed then pack and freeze the duckling along with the apples in one container and the juices in another. Thaw overnight at cool room temperature then reheat juices and complete as in basic recipe. Pack and freeze the ice cream as directed in the recipe. It will keep for up to three months.

INDEX